RAND NATIONAL DEFENSE RESEARCH INSTITUTE

Follow the Money

Promoting Greater Transparency in Department of Defense Security Cooperation Reporting

Beth Grill, Michael J. McNerney, Jeremy Boback, Renanah Miles,
Cynthia Clapp-Wincek, David E. Thaler

Prepared for the Office of the Secretary of Defense

Approved for public release; distribution unlimited

For more information on this publication, visit www.rand.org/t/RR2039

Library of Congress Cataloging-in-Publication Data is available for this publication.
ISBN: 978-0-8330-9910-5

Published by the RAND Corporation, Santa Monica, Calif.

Cover: AdobeStock.

Preface

The scope of the Department of Defense's (DoD's) engagement in security cooperation has expanded significantly over the past decade as Congress has authorized new programs to develop partner military capabilities, build relationships, and facilitate contingency and peacetime access to U.S. forces to meet an ever-widening set of U.S. national security objectives. Yet, there is currently no effective means for tracking spending on security cooperation activities. DoD lacks the detailed financial data necessary to respond to new congressional reporting requirements. Moreover, DoD leaders are unable to compare security cooperation spending across countries, regions, and programs, which is critical to future prioritization and resourcing decisions.

This report addresses the challenges of tracking security cooperation funding and program reporting by mapping out the data collection and reporting process of five security programs, analyzing current barriers, and describing how DoD and other agencies that collect data on foreign assistance activities have overcome some of these barriers. It then offers recommendations for streamlining the security cooperation reporting processes in preparation for meeting new requirements under the 2017 National Defense Authorization Act.

The findings of this report should be of interest to policymakers and stakeholders in the broader security cooperation arena in the Office of the Secretary of Defense; the Defense Security Cooperation Agency; the regional combatant commands; and the related service components, planners, program managers, and financial managers in the departments of Defense and State, as well as to congressional staffs that deal with security assistance to partner nations. Nongovernmental organizations involved in foreign aid may also find the report to be of interest.

This research was sponsored by the Deputy Assistant Secretary of Defense for Security Cooperation and was conducted within the International Security and Defense Policy Center of the RAND National Defense Research Institute, a federally funded research and development center sponsored by the Office of the Secretary of Defense, the Joint Staff, the Unified Combatant Commands, the Navy, the Marine Corps, the defense agencies, and the defense Intelligence Community.

For more information on the International Security and Defense Policy Center, see www.rand.org/nsrd/ndri/centers/isdp or contact the director (contact information is provided on the web page).

Contents

Figures and Tables

Figures

Tables

Summary

The U.S. government spends billions of dollars on security cooperation activities with foreign militaries and defense institutions each year. These engagements with foreign partners are an integral element of U.S. national security policy.[1] Yet DoD does not have a comprehensive mechanism for accounting for its security cooperation activities and for collecting detailed financial data. To date, there has been little analysis of the barriers that DoD faces in tracking security cooperation spending and the steps that will need to be taken to both meet new reporting requirements and to inform future DoD resourcing decisions. This report helps fill this gap.[2]

Security cooperation encompasses a broad range of DoD interactions with both foreign defense and nonmilitary security forces. It includes activities designed to develop partner defense and security capabilities and capacity for self-defense and multinational operations, provide U.S. forces with peacetime and contingency access to host nations, build defense relationships that promote specific U.S. security

---

1 Department of Defense (DoD) Directive 5132.03, *DoD Guidance for Security Cooperation*, Washington, D.C.: U.S. Department of Defense, August 29, 2016; Public Law 114–328, National Defense Authorization Act for Fiscal Year 2017, December 23, 2016.

2 The report builds on previous RAND research, including David E. Thaler, Michael J. McNerney, Beth Grill, Jefferson P. Marquis, Amanda Kadlec, *From Patchwork to Framework: A Review of Title 10 Authorities for Security Cooperation*, Santa Monica, Calif.: RAND Corporation, RR-1438-OSD, 2016, and Jefferson P. Marquis, Michael J. McNerney, S. Rebecca Zimmerman, Merrie Archer, Jeremy Boback, and David Stebbins, *Developing an Assessment, Monitoring, and Evaluation Framework for U.S. Department of Defense Security Cooperation*, Santa Monica, Calif.: RAND Corporation, RR-1611-OSD, 2016.

interests, or take other actions in support of U.S. objectives.[3] These activities are considered essential to enabling the United States to work "with allies and partners to deter, deny, and—when necessary—defeat potential state adversaries [while concurrently] leading multiple coalition efforts to disrupt, degrade, and defeat VEOs [Violent Extremist Organizations]."[4] DoD's engagement in security cooperation includes activities authorized under U.S. Code Title 10, which relates to the roles and missions of U.S. armed forces (such as U.S. military contacts and exercises), and under U.S. Code Title 22, which concerns foreign relations. The Title 22 activities are managed by the U.S. Department of State (DoS) but executed by DoD;[5] these activities, often referred to as *security assistance*, include foreign military sales and international military education and training.

The scope of DoD's involvement in security cooperation has greatly expanded over the past decade to meet evolving security challenges.[6] Congress has authorized dozens of new programs under U.S. Code Title 10, and related authorities, that enable the U.S. military to train, equip, and engage with partner nations to address a range of threats that includes global terrorism, failed states, the proliferation of weapons of mass destruction, narcotics trafficking, and ballistic missile threats.[7] Many of these new programs involve the provision of equipment, services, or other direct benefits to foreign populations, militaries, and governments. These activities qualify as foreign assistance, thus extending DoD's role in this subset of security cooperation that provides tangible or intangible benefits to foreign partners.

---

[3] DoD Directive 5132.03, 2016; 2017 National Defense Authorization Act (NDAA).

[4] Joint Chiefs of Staff, *The National Military Strategy of the United States of America 2015*, Washington, D.C.: U.S. Department of Defense, June 2015, p. 1.

[5] U.S. Code, Title 10, Armed Forces, undated; U.S. Code, Title 22, Foreign Relations and Intercourse.

[6] Joint Chiefs of Staff, 2015, p. 1.

[7] From previous RAND studies, we identified 176 individual security cooperation programs in effect in 2015; see Jennifer D. Moroney, David E. Thaler, and Joe Hogler, *Review of Security Cooperation Mechanisms Combatant Commands Utilize to Build Partner Capacity*, Santa Monica, Calif.: RAND Corporation, RR-413-OSD, 2013, and Thaler et al., 2016.

As DoD has assumed new responsibilities for engaging with foreign partners, it has become increasingly important to develop a means of tracking security cooperation activities. Both Congress and the public have required greater transparency in the reporting on DoD spending for security cooperation amid growing concerns over the accountability and effectiveness of foreign aid.[8] Since the United States became a signatory of the International Aid Transparency Initiative (IATI) in 2011, DoD has had the additional challenge of complying with international standards of reporting and public transparency for security cooperation activities that qualify as foreign assistance. At the same time, accounting for security cooperation spending has increasingly been viewed by DoD leaders as a critical first step to ensuring that U.S. security cooperation programs are effective and that DoD resources are appropriately aligned to meet U.S. strategic goals.

In 2017, pressure from Congress to improve security cooperation transparency has come to a head with the implementation of the Foreign Aid Transparency and Accountability Act of 2016 (P.L. 114-191), a bipartisan effort to increase foreign aid transparency, and the 2017 NDAA, which states that

> the Secretary of Defense should develop and maintain an assessment, monitoring, and evaluation framework . . . to inform security cooperation planning, policies, and resource decisions as well as ensure the effectiveness and efficiency of security cooperation efforts.[9]

---

[8] An Open Government Directive was signed by the Obama administration in 2009 to respond to public demand for transparency (Peter R. Orszag, "Open Government Directive," memorandum for the heads of executive departments and agencies, Washington, D.C., December 8, 2009). This was followed by international efforts, including the Paris Declaration on Aid Effectiveness and the Accra Agenda for Action in September 2011. See ForeignAssistance.gov, "About Aid Transparency," webpage, undated, and Organisation for Economic Co-operation and Development, "Paris Declaration and Accra Agenda for Action," undated. Congress has also has required DoD to provide greater transparency in foreign aid spending, culminating in the passage of the Foreign Aid Transparency and Accountability Act of 2016.

[9] 2017 NDAA, Section 1205, pp. 481–482.

President Donald Trump's businesslike approach to governing has also led to the support of a "return on investment" perspective within his administration, which calls for more-detailed accounting. Secretary of Defense James Mattis coauthored a 2016 report that explicitly expressed the concern that "we have not measured the ultimate costs of the outcomes we seek," a concern that certainly applies to security cooperation.[10] Thus, it seems likely that both Congress and the Trump administration will demand improved monitoring of security cooperation activities with the ultimate goal of evaluating the return on investment—or "bang for the buck"—from U.S. efforts to educate, train, equip, and exercise with foreign security forces. The question is, how will DoD be able to provide the necessary data on security cooperation when it lacks an effective mechanism to link the bangs and the bucks?

The current structure for administering security cooperation programs has made it exceedingly difficult to track funding and activities comprehensively. The security cooperation authorities that have been introduced over the last decade have created a patchwork of funding sources, program management structures, and data-collection systems. Although DoD has numerous systems to track security cooperation activities, refine and prioritize objectives, and plan and document expenditures, these systems are disconnected from each other, lack sufficient detail, and are often incomplete. In particular, DoD's planning, program management, and financial accounting systems are disjointed, resulting in "cylinders of excellence" that make it extremely challenging to link the disbursement of resources with activities and planning objectives. While the problem of accounting for the disbursement of funds for particular activities is DoD wide, it is uniquely challenging for security cooperation programs.[11]

---

[10] James O. Ellis Jr., James N. Mattis, and Kori Schake, "Restoring Our National Security," in George P. Shultz, ed., *Blueprint for America*, Stanford, Calif.: Hoover Institution, 2016.

[11] DoD has been unable to meet a 1997 congressional requirement to prepare audited financial statements. The agency is currently working to respond to a Financial Improvement and Audit Readiness (FIAR) requirement from the 2010 NDAA to ensure that its consolidated financial statements are audit ready by September 30, 2017. While DoD has made significant progress in implementing its FIAR guidance, the U.S. Government Accountability Office

In an effort to meet the external transparency requirements that Congress and IATI have imposed and to meet equally important internal requirements for assessment, monitoring, and evaluation, DoD has attempted to develop stronger security cooperation reporting standards in recent years, yet, to date, these efforts have largely been ad hoc and have not been conducted in a comprehensive manner. [12] The development of the Global Theater Security Cooperation Management Information System (G-TSCMIS) software platform has helped improve event planning and tracking of the execution of security cooperation activities but has not provided an effective means for tracking resources or for linking program data with financial data.[13]

While the bar for reporting continues to rise, DoD program and financial offices still do not systematically collect and analyze security cooperation funding data by country and rarely collect detailed activity-level information. Meeting new demands for transparency will require DoD to revolutionize how it manages funding for security cooperation programs because it will need to develop new, systematic ways to collect and integrate data across multiple management organizations and financial, programming, and information systems.

Our research considered the process of security cooperation programs as they existed in 2016 and early 2017 and sought to address

---

(GAO) has indicated that the process has not yet resulted in a fundamental transformation of systems and operations necessary to resolve the department's long-standing financial management deficiencies. See Office of the Under Secretary of Defense (Comptroller)/Chief Financial Officer, *Financial Improvement and Audit Readiness (FIAR) Plan Status Report*, Washington, D.C.: U.S. Department of Defense, May 2016; GAO, *High-Risk Series: Progress on Many High-Risk Areas, While Substantial Efforts Needed on Others*, Washington, D.C., GAO-17-317, February 2017; GAO, *DoD Financial Management: Greater Visibility Needed to Better Assess Audit Readiness for Property, Plant, and Equipment*, Washington, D.C., GAO-16-383, May 2016a.

[12] DoD Instruction 5132.14, *Assessment, Monitoring, and Evaluation Policy for the Security Cooperation Enterprise*, January 13, 2017; Marquis et al., 2016.

[13] Jefferson P. Marquis, David E. Thaler, S. Rebecca Zimmerman, Megan Stewart, and Jeremy Boback, *The Global-Theater Security Cooperation Management Information System Assessment and Implications for Strategic Users*, Santa Monica, Calif.: RAND Corporation, 2016, Not available to the general public.

many of the issues that DoD will face in meeting new reporting requirements. In this report, we attempt to answer the following questions:

- What are the drivers for transparency in security cooperation program reporting?
- What are the barriers to collecting data on security cooperation programs?
- What practices have been developed in DoD to overcome these barriers?
- What lessons can be learned from other agencies' efforts to improve transparency in foreign assistance reporting?
- How can DoD improve compliance with transparency requirements and streamline the reporting process?

This report addresses these questions in four ways. First, we provide a basis for understanding and managing the significant effort that will be required to track detailed data on U.S. security cooperation spending to meet new reporting requirements. These efforts will likely require an investment in resources and manpower to collect activity-level information and to link existing data systems. Second, we help clarify the requirements for reporting on DoD's foreign assistance activities and what the United States can and cannot report to public websites, which may help DoD develop the appropriate caveats to its reporting and provide more realistic expectations for transparency for both internal and external audiences. Third, we identify the need to develop linkages between planning, program, and financial offices and provided examples of steps to create closer ties both within DoD and with other agencies. We also provide suggestions for information technology (IT) solutions to facilitate these connections. Fourth, we provide evidence for the need for better tracking of financial data to meet internal and external requirements, which will not only help to encourage closer engagement in the data collection process but will also aid in the prioritization of resources and activities.

Approach

Our objective was to assess both DoD reporting on its foreign assistance activities to IATI and its reporting on security cooperation activities more broadly. We started by reviewing congressional and IATI reporting requirements and recent DoD reporting to the online database of U.S. foreign aid—the Foreign Assistance Dashboard—from which all U.S. agencies submit data to IATI, then conducted a gap analysis to assess the extent to which DoD reporting is meeting current IATI standards.[14] We then conducted semistructured interviews with U.S. defense officials involved in collecting security cooperation data, including program managers, database managers, and financial managers across the DoD enterprise to inquire about the data that they collect. This was followed by focused discussions with U.S. officials in DoS, the U.S. Agency for International Development (USAID), and the Foreign Assistance Dashboard to learn about the foreign aid reporting processes that they have developed to track foreign aid data. We also conducted semistructured interviews with nongovernment transparency organizations, including IATI, Publish What You Fund, and Open Society, to gain an understanding of the ways that they rate the transparency efforts of DoD and other national and international agencies

Drawing from this research, we mapped out the reporting processes of five of the 13 security cooperation programs reported to the Foreign Assistance Dashboard: Overseas Humanitarian Disaster and Civic Aid, Global Train and Equip, the Combating Terrorism Fellowship Program (CTFP), Counternarcotics (CN), and Cooperative Threat Reduction (CTR). These programs were chosen, with the advice of our sponsor, to reflect a cross section of programs being reported to the dashboard in terms of their reporting requirements, sources of funding, and management structures.[15] We analyzed the comprehensiveness of congressional reporting requirements for each program, how

[14] The Foreign Assistance Dashboard is also known as ForeignAssistance.gov.

[15] These five programs were not intended to be representative of all DoD's security cooperation programs but only to illustrate some of the common issues for a range of programs.

well program and financial management communities were linked for data collection, and the level and type of data collected, as well as the databases used to manage program and financial data for each. We also looked at lessons drawn from DoS and USAID efforts to improve data collection on foreign assistance reporting and considered the recommendations from nongovernmental organizations for improving DoD transparency.

Analysis Revealed Ways DoD Might Overcome Barriers to Transparency

There several barriers to collecting program and financial data on security cooperation programs:

- Security cooperation programs are based on a patchwork of authorities.
- Planning, program, and financial communities operate separately and without a common set of clear reporting standards.
- Financial data are not consistently defined, tracked, or reported; reported data are rarely reconciled or verified.

These barriers help explain why it has been so difficult for DoD to meet transparency requirements.

In reviewing the five existing programs, we found that DoD program managers have developed a number of ad hoc measures to meet congressional reporting requirements in the past that have created better linkages between communities, allowed the collection of more-detailed data, and improved integration of program and financial data. Not surprisingly, we found the most innovative and far-reaching practices were developed internally for the programs with the most stringent congressional reporting requirements. While each program has met its reporting requirements in the past, the programs that were required to provide particularly detailed data in their annual reports to

Congress were forced to develop more-extensive mechanisms for tracking and collecting data across systems.[16]

Table S.1 highlights how each of the five programs we analyzed has met congressional reporting requirements, using four criteria we assessed to be important for facilitating transparency: the comprehensiveness of existing reporting requirements, the degree of linkage between communities that were developed, the level of detail of data collected, and the degree to which databases integrate program and financial data. Chapter Three discusses the contents in more detail, but the table is useful here for illustrating several mechanisms for collecting better security cooperation program and funding data. For example, the CN program developed a specialized database to track activities by type and country using project codes. CTFP employed program coordinators to collect data across each of the combatant commands. And the CTR program utilized the Program Budget Management Tool (PBMT) on a SharePoint site to integrate program and financial data, which serves as a common point of reference for all offices both for completing external reports and for conducting internal program reviews.

We coded each of five programs based on degree of transparency, from light to dark. The lightest shade of blue for congressional reporting, for example, indicates the least extensive reporting requirements, while the darkest blue represents the most comprehensive requirements (e.g., the requirement to provide detailed information on the disbursement of funds by country and activity). For degree of integration, the darkest shade of blue represents the highest degree of integration of program and financial data. While many of these practices are designed to overcome the unique barriers each individual program faces and cannot be applied to all programs, they may provide a model for future data collection and integration. The practices highlighted in the report are outlined in red in Table S.1.

---

16 Appendix C in the companion document (available at http://www.rand.org/pubs/research_reports/RR2039.html) provides more-detailed analysis of reporting requirments for each of the five programs.

Table S.1
How Select Security Cooperation Programs Meet Current Congressional Reporting Requirements

	OHDACA	GT&E	CN	CTFP	CTR
Comprehensiveness of reporting requirements	Total obligations Number of missions	Notifications Assessments	Biannual expenditures by country and activity type	Expenditures by country and activity After-action reports	Notifications Obligations, expenditures, and plans by country and activity
Degree of linkage between communities	Proposal process	Case adjustment process	DoD Inspector General's report	CTFP Manager	DTRA connections
Level of detail of data collected	Projects planned Estimated costs CCMD allocations	Building partner capacity cases Equipment delivery Training	CN activity by country Project code	Students, courses by country, assessments	Planned, executed activities by country
Degree to which databases integrate program and financial data	OHASIS	SCIP SANWeb	CN Database	SANWeb	PBMT SharePoint

SOURCE: Discussions with DoD officials.

NOTES: DTRA = Defense Threat Reduction Agency; CCMD = combatant command; OHASIS = Overseas Humanitarian Assistance Shared Information System; SCIP = Security Cooperation Information Portal; SANWeb = Security Assistance Network Web Tool. Dark blue indicates greatest level of detail required for congressional reporting, most significant linkages between communities, comprehensive data collection on disbursements, or highest degree of integration of program and financial data, depending on the row. Cells outlined in red indicate practices highlighted in this report.

Other agencies offer important lessons on how the process might be improved. DoS and USAID have made significant efforts toward increasing transparency in foreign assistance reporting. USAID created a technical working group that developed a multiyear IATI Cost Management Plan to improve reporting to IATI.[17] DoS subsequently established its own working group to undertake a foreign assistance data review to better utilize its budget, financial, and program management systems to track or report on foreign assistance programs or funds at the level needed for recent transparency, congressional, or management purposes.[18] Their experience demonstrates the importance of pursuing a comprehensive plan for improving the reporting process by establishing working groups that bring together programming, budgeting, and IT personnel and developing clearly defined reporting requirements and a common coding system across offices, as well as a systematic procedure for vetting and redacting sensitive or classified data.

The mechanisms that DoD program managers have developed and practices that have evolved from USAID and DoS transparency efforts may prove increasingly valuable as DoD faces higher expectations for producing detailed financial data on its security cooperation programs to meet IATI requirements and new congressional mandates arising from the Foreign Aid Transparency and Accountability Act and the 2017 NDAA and a potentially more business-minded administration that demands greater insight into return on investment.

Short- and Long-Term Recommendations for DoD

These findings suggest a number of recommendations for improving the process of tracking security cooperation funding and reporting that will strengthen DoD compliance with IATI and prepare to meet new requirements for security cooperation transparency.

---

17 USAID, *International Aid Transparency Initiative (IATI) Cost Management Plan*, Washington, D.C., June 2015b.

18 DoS, *Foreign Assistance Data Review: Phase Two—Data Element Index*, Winter 2016.

For the short term, we suggest focusing on improving the quality and consistency of reporting existing data. Our short-term recommendations are directed at the Office of the Secretary of Defense (OSD), which currently has the primary role in reporting to the Foreign Assistance Dashboard. We recommend that OSD

- *Define the scope of foreign assistance and security cooperation reporting to internal and external audiences, including principled exceptions for national security.* Clarifying which DoD activities qualify as security cooperation, the subset of these activities that qualify as foreign assistance, and the limits to the public releasability of data may make it possible to create more-realistic expectations for security cooperation reporting.
- *Institute a process for validating information and vetting it for releasability.* The development of an internal process for validating data across DoD offices and conducting a security review before data are released can provide more credible and secure reporting.
- *Consolidate the data-collection process by using a shared reporting template and align tasks for collecting data for the Foreign Assistance Dashboard with data required by the 2017 NDAA.* By utilizing a single online site for all DoD offices to provide security cooperation information for submission to the dashboard and other future requirements, OSD may be able to facilitate the process for more frequent and comprehensive data reporting.
- *Establish a working group across program, financial, and information offices within DoD to develop a common understanding of transparency requirements, and a process for developing new reporting standards and mechanisms for collecting data.* A policy-level working group that draws from the leadership of program, financial, and IT offices, as well as the Joint Staff and the Defense Security Cooperation Agency (DSCA), would provide critical input and buy-in to achieve a long-term, integrated solution. Discussions should include ways to incorporate activity data G-TSCMIS tracks with resource data that DoD financial systems collect.

Our longer-term recommendations focus on the development of new tracking processes. They are targeted to DSCA, the organization that has traditionally administered all the DoD security assistance activities through which the U.S. government furnishes defense articles, military training, and other services to foreign militaries and that will, according to the stipulations of the 2017 NDAA, assume responsibility for managing and reporting on security cooperation programs. We recommend that DSCA

- *Consolidate security cooperation administrative and reporting process, incorporating workarounds and best practices and delegating responsibilities to offices that have developed methods for meeting new requirements.* As DSCA assumes responsibility for managing a wide portfolio of security cooperation programs, it may leverage some of the innovative practices for collecting data that the Global Train and Equip, CN, CTFP, and the CTR program more broadly have adopted. At the same time, it may be beneficial to allow some offices to continue to collect data using current processes for the immediate future to maintain the benefits of existing workarounds.
- *Building from the OSD working group recommended above, establish standing working groups of key security cooperation stakeholders from the program, financial, and information management communities to develop common reporting standards and mechanisms for collecting and reporting security cooperation program data.* Standing working groups could create key linkages between DSCA program offices, the combatant commands, implementing agencies (which include the services and the Defense Threat Reduction Agency) and security cooperation offices that work directly with partner nations, to engage them in the development of new reporting standards and data-collection processes. While OSD will likely maintain oversight of security cooperation policy, DSCA could organize these groups to complement working groups established at the policy level, as recommended above.
- *Develop consistent financial data requirements for tracking transactions across military departments, agencies, and contracting organiza-*

tions. Build on DoD's new Defense Agency Initiative accounting system to develop common identifiers for security cooperation-related financial transactions across military departments, agencies, and contracting organizations.

- *Incorporate common business rules for security cooperation reporting, establishing country codes that can be used across financial and program systems.* An effective tracking system will require that all offices use the same coding system for reporting on security cooperation activities.
- *Define new roles for staff to manage data collection at the regional and country levels.* To achieve the level of detailed reporting to meet new NDAA requirements, it will be necessary to obtain more information from security cooperation offices or implementing agencies. This may require an additional investment in manpower and resources.
- *Provide a central location from which to draw financial data for reporting.* Modeled on the DoS's data warehouse, which serves as the repository for transactional data drawn from the enterprise-wide DoS financial system from which all of the department's foreign aid reporting is drawn. DoD could assign dedicated budget analysts to pull data from DoD accounting systems for all security cooperation reporting.[19]
- *Consider IT solutions for linking program and financial data.* One option would be to develop of a software tool that allows data from DoD accounting systems to be matched to data collected through G-TSCMIS.

Implications of This Research

This report does not provide a comprehensive analysis of DoD reporting on all security cooperation activities or provide a definitive solution for tracking funding data across all DoD's various program and

---

[19] U.S. Department of State, Bureau of the Comptroller and Global Financial Services, *Fiscal Year 2014 Agency Financial Report*, November 2014.

accounting systems. Instead, it is intended to serve as a first step toward improving transparency of DoD security cooperation programs by providing an overview of the challenges that DoD faces in meeting transparency requirements and possible approaches to improving the process of data reporting.

Illuminating the process for gathering better data on DoD security cooperation activities has five potential benefits. First, DoD will not only improve its compliance with IATI standards and provide greater transparency to the international community of donors but may also set an example for other nations' military organizations or ministries of defense and gain greater cooperation from foreign partners in both foreign assistance and broader security cooperation missions the future. Second, DoD will be able to provide greater transparency on funding of security cooperation programs to other U.S. government agencies and the public, which provides a better understanding of DoD activities and its interactions with foreign partners to U.S. taxpayers. Third, this research will enable DoD to respond to new congressional requirements for detailed data on its activities that go beyond what is reported publicly. The data will be critical for Congress to see where and how its appropriations have been spent and begin to answer questions about value of its investments, which in turn will impact DoD funding. Fourth, the research will provide U.S. military officials in the field with better information on how their resources are being spent, which can be helpful in determining execution rates and generating more-accurate estimates for planning.

Finally, and perhaps most importantly, better tracking of program and financial data will provide DoD policymakers with information on where and how their limited security cooperation funding is being spent and ultimately how they should make future resourcing decisions. The risk of not having the data is that DoD policymakers will not be able to prioritize security cooperation engagements most effectively to meet U.S. national security objectives.[20]

---

[20] Tommy Ross, "Leveraging Security Cooperation as Military Strategy," *Washington Quarterly*, Fall 2016.

Acknowledgments

The authors are grateful for the support and help of many individuals. First and foremost, we would like to thank our sponsor, former Deputy Assistant Secretary of Defense for Security Cooperation Tommy Ross, for his insight and guidance. We benefited from his wealth of experience and interest in exploring the wider implications of transparency in security cooperation reporting. We are also grateful to Nathan Bein, our point of contact, who provided us with invaluable direction and assistance, and to Principal Director Leslie Hunter for her support throughout the course of our research.

We are indebted to the many officials at the combatant and component commands and to DoD stakeholders in the Washington, D.C., area, who were so gracious with their time in explaining the processes they use to collect and report security cooperation information and providing us with their ideas on how the process might be improved. We also thank officials at the Department of State and the U.S. Agency for International Development for sharing their experiences in working toward improving transparency in foreign assistance reporting, as well as officials in nongovernmental organizations that are dedicated to promoting transparency for sharing their insight and perspective with us.

Many thanks go to RAND colleagues Christopher Paul and Jefferson Marquis for their careful, thoughtful reviews of the draft document. Their critiques greatly strengthened this report. Finally, we appreciate the support to our colleague Maria Falvo in preparing the draft for review.

Of course, responsibility for the content of this report lies solely with the authors.

CHAPTER ONE

Introduction

The U.S. Department of Defense's (DoD's) engagement in security cooperation activities with its foreign partners has increased significantly since 2001. Cooperation with foreign partners has become integral to DoD's mission to achieve U.S. strategic objectives. Congress has enacted a multitude of new laws to address security challenges ranging from "violent extremist organizations that are undermining transregional security to revisionist states that are challenging international norms."[1] Laws have been introduced affecting not only U.S. Code Title 22 (22 USC), which concerns foreign relations activities overseen by the U.S. Department of State (DoS), but also 10 USC, which relates to the role of the Armed Forces. These laws have provided the military with greater authority to develop partner defense and security capabilities and capacity for self-defense and multinational operations, as well as to gain or maintain peacetime and contingency access to host nations, build defense relationships that promote specific U.S. security interests, and take other actions in support of U.S. objectives.[2] With

---

[1] Joint Chiefs of Staff, *The National Military Strategy of the United States of America 2015*, Washington, D.C.: U.S. Department of Defense, June 2015.

[2] Several security cooperation programs have also been introduced under 50 USC (War and National Defense) and under 6 USC (Domestic Security). See David E. Thaler, Michael J. McNerney, Beth Grill, Jefferson P. Marquis, and Amanda Kadlec, *From Patchwork to Framework: A Review of Title 10 Authorities for Security Cooperation*, Santa Monica, Calif.: RAND Corporation, RR-1438-OSD, 2016; DoD Directive 5132.03, *DoD Guidance for Security Cooperation*, Washington, D.C.: U.S. Department of Defense, August 29, 2016; and Public Law (P.L.) 114–328, National Defense Authorization Act for Fiscal Year 2017, December 23, 2016 (the FY 2017 NDAA).

this expanded authority, DoD has assumed both the responsibility for managing an increasingly complex set of security cooperation programs and for tracking and reporting the thousands of activities these programs support.

DoD officials now manage thousands of security cooperation activities each year through as many as 176 different security cooperation programs.[3] These programs include Foreign Military Sales (FMS) and International Military Education and Training, which provide traditional security assistance to foreign partners under Title 22 authorities, and new partnership capacity-building activities introduced through the Title 10 Global Train and Equip (GT&E) program and the Afghanistan Security Forces Fund, which provide tangible support for partner nations and are considered to be "foreign assistance." The list also includes a number of programs that are not designed to provide any direct benefits to partners, such as Joint Combined Exercises and Training and information-sharing and relationship-building activities, and would not be categorized as foreign assistance. The management of security cooperation programs has also become increasingly challenging with the introduction of multiple planning, executing, and funding processes and information systems, as well as various types of reporting requirements. This in turn has made it difficult for DoD to collect comprehensive data on its ever-widening set of and security cooperation engagements.

The growth in complexity of DoD's security cooperation activities has occurred in parallel with an increasing interest in transparency in government over the past decade and the introduction of open government policies. The 2009 Office of Management and Budget (OMB) Open Government Directive required all U.S. government agencies to

---

[3] Working from previous RAND studies, we identified 176 individual security cooperation programs that were in effect in 2015. Many of these programs were consolidated with the passage of the FY 2017 NDAA (P.L. 114–328), which created a single multipurpose authority to build the capacity of foreign security forces under 10 USC 333, Foreign Security Forces: Authority to Build Capacity. See Jennifer D. Moroney, David E. Thaler, and Joe Hogler, *Review of Security Cooperation Mechanisms Combatant Commands Utilize to Build Partner Capacity*, Santa Monica, Calif.: RAND Corporation, RR-413-OSD, 2013, and Thaler et al., 2016.

create open government websites and open government plans to support greater public awareness and accountability in government spending.[4] During the Obama administration, there was particular interest in transparency in foreign aid to improve its efficacy for development and to encourage greater accountability among international partners. In January 2009, the United States initiated an effort to improve aid effectiveness in accordance with the Paris Declaration on Aid Effectiveness and U.S. G8 and G20 commitments.[5]

These efforts led the U.S. government to establish new mechanisms for reporting U.S. assistance, most notably the Foreign Assistance Dashboard, which was established in 2010 to provide an online database of U.S. government spending on foreign aid.[6] The following year, the United States made a further commitment to international foreign assistance transparency by signing on to the International Aid Transparency Initiative (IATI), a voluntary effort organized by foreign aid donors, recipient countries, and civil society organizations to improve aid effectiveness and accountability. Through IATI, the United States committed to publishing up-to-date foreign assistance data on an online registry using a common standard format for reporting on the allocation of funds and the results of aid programs. While U.S. government officials, partner nations, and international nongovernmental organizations (NGOs) hailed the dashboard—also known as ForeignAssistance.gov—and the IATI online registry as important avenues for transparency, they have placed new demands for data collection and reporting on the 22 U.S. government agencies that publish

---

4 Peter R. Orszag, "Open Government Directive," memorandum for the heads of executive departments and agencies, Washington, D.C., December 8, 2009.

5 Organisation for Economic Co-operation and Development (OECD), "Paris Declaration and Accra Agenda for Action," undated, and OMB, "Guidance on Collection of U.S. Foreign Assistance Data," Washington, D.C., Bulletin 12-01, September 25, 2012. We refer to this in text as Bulletin 12-01.

6 The Foreign Assistance Dashboard is also known as ForeignAssistance.gov. The dashboard requires 20 U.S. government agencies to monitor and valuate all foreign aid programs and improve transparency by publicly sharing performance data.

foreign aid data regarding the type of assistance and level of funding the agencies provide to foreign partners.[7]

DoD faces particular challenges regarding its participation in international transparency initiatives, compared with providers of development aid. While many of DoD's engagements with other nations include providing tangible or intangible resources to a foreign country or international organization, some activities are intended solely for the benefit of the United States. The purpose of security cooperation is to promote U.S. security interests and is often closely linked to U.S. operational demands (such as obtaining information, access, or situational awareness in foreign countries), and the line between foreign assistance and U.S. military operations can be difficult to delineate. Because the classification and sensitivity of U.S. military engagements can affect the safety of both U.S. and partner forces, DoD also faces significant restrictions on the types of data it can provide to open forums. Moreover, DoD as an organization has had perennial problems tracking security cooperation activities and information.

These challenges, combined with the daunting scope and scale of DoD activities around the world, make it especially challenging for DoD to report its activities to the Foreign Assistance Dashboard and IATI and to meet the growing number of transparency requirements imposed through U.S. government directives and government agency reporting, such as U.S. Government Accountability Office (GAO) reports. Congress has imposed new, more-extensive reporting requirements since 2014. The Digital Accountability and Transparency Act requires governmentwide standards for tracking federal funds and publishing spending information on USASpending.gov.[8] The Foreign Aid Transparency and Accountability Act requires U.S. government

[7] Mark Tran, "Hillary Clinton Declares US Support for Aid Initiative," *Guardian*, November 11, 2011; Modernizing Foreign Assistance Network, "MFAN Statement: Sec. Clinton Speech in Busan Reaffirms U.S. Commitment to Aid Effectiveness," November 30, 2011; U.S. Agency for International Development (USAID), "Aid Transparency Country Pilot Assessment," Final Report, May 2015a.

[8] P.L. 113-110, Digital Accountability and Transparency Act of 2014, May 9, 2014, Sec. 2.

agencies to closely monitor and evaluate all foreign aid programs.[9] Moreover, the FY 2017 NDAA (P.L. 114–328) includes some of the most stringent reporting requirements for security cooperation to date (see Table 1.1).

These increasing external requirements for transparency have occurred at the same time as DoD leaders are seeking to obtain more-detailed data on security cooperation programs to enable comparing security cooperation spending across countries, regions, and programs, which is critical to future prioritization and resourcing decisions. Yet

Table 1.1
Reporting Requirements of the FY 2017 NDAA

Section	Reporting Requirements	Frequency of Reporting	Start Date
Annual report	Cost and expenditures of each security cooperation program Description of program Participation of partner-nation security forces Percentage of U.S. forces	Annually	January 2018
Budget	Obligations and expenditures	Quarterly	FY 2017
Monitoring reports	Status of funds allocated: unobligated funds, unliquidated obligations Disbursements by recipient country	Quarterly	FY 2017
Train-and-equip proposals	Amount, type, and purpose of security assistance provided to country during three preceding FYs	Before initiating activity	FY 2017
Quadrennial review[a]	Review of security assistance programs, authorities, and resources—and alignment with policy objectives	Every four years	January 2018
Annual budget	Identify funds necessary for implementing security cooperation programs and activities with appropriate justification	Annually	FY 2018

SOURCES: 2017 NDAA and discussions with DoD officials.

[a] Presidential review.

---

[9] P.L. 114-191, Foreign Aid Transparency and Accountability Act of 2016, July 15, 2016, Sec. 3.

the current structure for administering security cooperation programs has made it exceedingly difficult to track funding and activities comprehensively. Meeting such demands for transparency and accountability will require DoD to revolutionize how it manages funding and program information for security cooperation programs.

To support DoD's efforts to improve its ability to meet current and future demands for improved security cooperation reporting, the RAND Corporation was asked to assess DoD compliance with its IATI obligations and to recommend ways to streamline security cooperation reporting more broadly. As part of this research effort, we sought to answer five questions:

- What are the drivers for transparency in security cooperation program reporting?
- What are the barriers for collecting data on security cooperation programs?
- What practices has DoD developed to overcome these barriers?
- What lessons can be learned from other agencies' efforts to improve transparency in foreign assistance reporting?
- How can DoD improve compliance with transparency requirements and streamline the reporting process?

Internal and External Drivers of Transparency in DoD Security Cooperation Reporting

Since 2016, DoD has been driven to meet new transparency requirements that Congress and other external government agencies have set. At the same time, DoD has faced increasing pressure collect data to meet its own internal requirements for the purposes of accountability and strategic prioritization. Section 1202 of the FY 2016 NDAA (P.L. 112-239) required the Secretary of Defense, in coordination with the Secretary of State, to develop a strategic framework for security cooperation to guide prioritization of resources and activities. While many individual DoD program managers and combatant command (CCMD) planners have the visibility they need to prioritize security cooperation efforts within their limited scope of responsibility, a strategic framework to guide prioritization at the level of the whole DoD enterprise requires senior DoD leaders to have greater access to financial information on security cooperation programs to ensure that the disbursement of funds align with U.S. strategic objectives and are used most effectively across all geographic commands.

Section 1241 of the FY 2017 NDAA dramatically restructured the legislative authorities governing security cooperation and strengthened the requirements for DoD to monitor resources and activities and evaluate their effectiveness. For example, this provision required the Secretary of Defense and the Secretary of State to jointly design many of the programs that train and equip foreign militaries. Such coordination requirements drive an ever-greater need for detailed information on security cooperation programs at all levels of the government. Table 1.1 highlights some of the Section 1241 resourcing and programmatic reporting requirements.

While our research was designed to focus on the Foreign Assistance Dashboard and IATI requirements for foreign assistance reporting, it is important to recognize that there are a number of other external drivers of transparency in the funding of security cooperation programs. As Figure 1.1 highlights, partner nations have played a role in requesting greater transparency in U.S. security cooperation engagements; U.S. government agencies have required a closer accounting of U.S. funding; and Congress has placed new requirements for reporting on the disbursement of funds and their impact on U.S. national security. Meanwhile, open government reporting requirements adopted under the Obama administration continue to require publication of data to open sources, and the new administration will likely require even more transparency to demonstrate "return on investment." DoD leaders will also require more detailed information on security cooperation what could be considered "internal transparency" in the future.

As Figure 1.2 shows, the most important drivers of transparency may be internal to DoD. Efforts to improve country-level planning, assessments, monitoring, and evaluation require a clear understanding of partner-country capabilities and security challenges, resource allocation, program performance, and effectiveness in advancing U.S.

Figure 1.1
External Drivers of Transparency

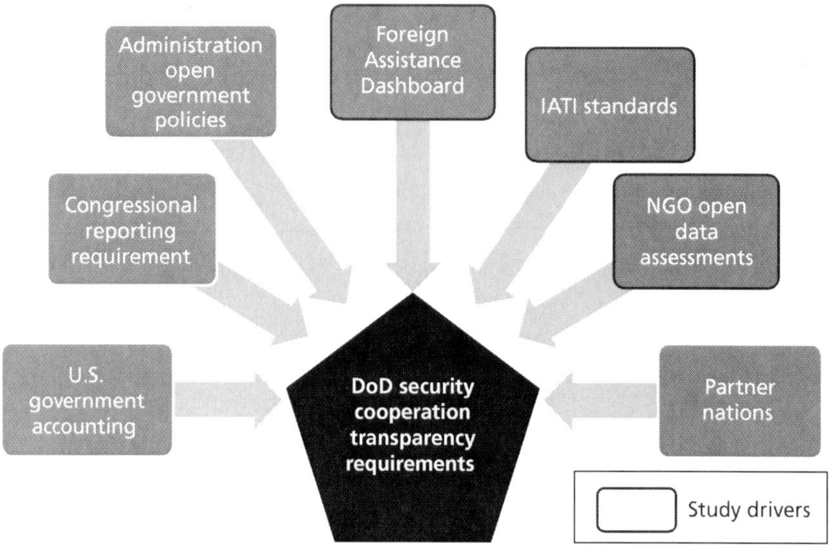

RAND *RR2039-1.1*

objectives. CCMD planning drives similar requirements but relies on aggregated data across multiple countries to evaluate how security cooperation activities support lines of effort for various regional missions, such as maritime security, counterterrorism (CT), counternarcotics (CN), and counterproliferation. Program managers in DoD headquarters components must also aggregate data, often globally, to evaluate how their programs perform against senior leader objectives.

The Office of the Secretary of Defense (OSD) and the Joint Staff have the most challenging task: analyzing data across countries, regions, and programs to fulfill the oversight responsibilities of the Secretary of Defense and Chairman of the Joint Chiefs of Staff. Maximizing the department's return on investment means advancing U.S. national security interests while minimizing the burden on American taxpayers. These internal requirements may, in fact, be more extensive than the external requirements described earlier. Meeting them demands detailed data on security cooperation activities to determine where and how security cooperation funds are being spent to support

Figure 1.2
Internal DoD Drivers of Transparency

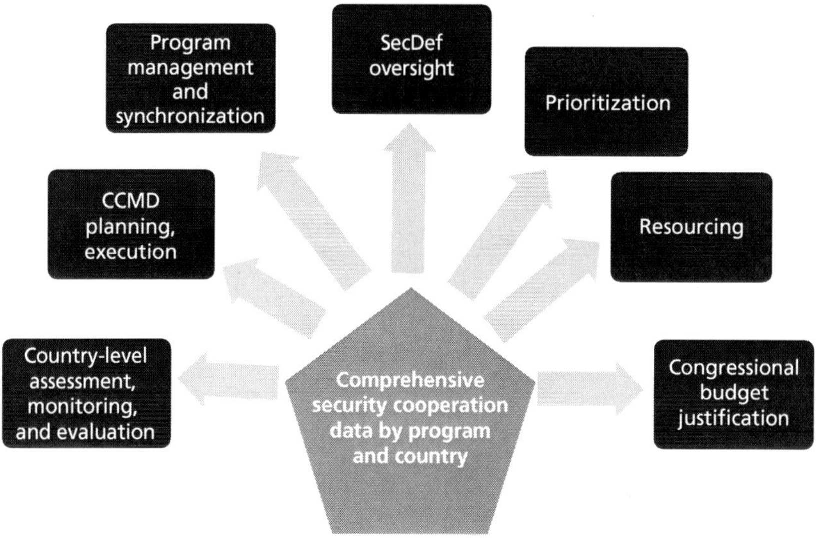

RAND *RR2039-1.2*

rigorous prioritization of countries, programs, and the resources that go into them.

Stovepipes between planning offices make it exceedingly difficult for leaders at all levels of DoD to develop situational awareness, improve efficiency, make trade-offs, or even simply know what is working and what is not. The risks of not having sufficient insight into security cooperation programs and funding will be a significant loss of opportunity to engage effectively with foreign partners to enhance U.S. national security. The department's efforts to improve its collection and reporting of detailed cooperation data to meet external requirements may provide greater visibility to stakeholders across the board. Moreover, improving these may provide the first step toward developing effective assessment, monitoring, and evaluation of security cooperation programs in the future.

Methodology

This research was designed to assess DoD reporting on its foreign assistance activities to IATI and its reporting on security cooperation activities more broadly. Our objectives were to provide recommendations for streamlining DoD reporting that would extend beyond improving DoD compliance with IATI to meet more-comprehensive reporting requirements for DoD security cooperation spending.

We therefore began by reviewing IATI reporting requirements and conducting focused discussions with U.S. government officials involved with the Foreign Assistance Dashboard, which provides data to IATI, and with representatives of national and international nongovernment transparency organizations, including IATI and Publish What You Fund (PWYF), to learn about their reporting standards and rating criteria. We then conducted a gap analysis to assess the extent to which DoD reporting meets the requirements for the Foreign Assistance Dashboard, IATI, and the PWYF Aid Transparency Index (ATI) to gain an understanding of how DoD could improve its published ratings.

In the next phase of the research, we conducted an analysis of the data collection and reporting process of five security cooperation programs from among the 13 programs that were published on the Foreign Assistance Dashboard in 2016.[10] Our OSD sponsor selected the five programs to reflect a range of the programs reported at that time in terms of reporting requirements, funding sources, program administration, and data collection processes: Overseas Humanitarian Disaster and Civic Aid (OHDACA), GT&E, the Combating Terrorism Fellowship Program (CTFP), CN, and Cooperative Threat Reduction (CTR). These five programs were among the most comprehensive and

---

[10] The 13 programs were the Afghanistan Infrastructure Fund, the Afghanistan Security Forces Fund, the Coalition Readiness Support Fund, the Humanitarian and Civic Assistance portions of combatant commanders' Civil Affairs budgets, the Combatant Commander Initiative Fund, CTFP, the Commanders' Emergency Response Program, CTR, the Defense Health Program (the Armed Forces Health Surveillance Center, the surveillance and response portion for the Division of Global Emerging Infections, and DoD HIV/AIDS Prevention), GT&E, CN, the International Counterproliferation Program, and OHDACA.

enduring of the 13 (they did not include programs focused specifically on Afghanistan, for example) and were reflective of the diversity of security cooperation programs beyond those that were being reported to the dashboard. Given the wide range of security programs that exist, however, these five programs should not be considered representative of all 176 security cooperation programs that were in effect at the time.

To conduct our analysis, we organized a series of focused discussions with more than 60 defense officials involved in managing and tracking these security cooperation programs. We identified a wide range of DoD personnel from across OSD, the Joint Staff, the Defense Threat Reduction Agency (DTRA), and DoD's agency for security cooperation program management—the Defense Security Cooperation Agency (DSCA)—as well as several of the geographic CCMDs. We subsequently engaged with representatives of various policy, planning, program management, and financial management communities.[11] We also spoke with DoD security cooperation database managers (e.g., Global Theater Security Cooperation Management Information System [G-TSCMIS]) and those involved in database design and business management. Although we could not eliminate selection bias, we attempted to address these concerns by seeking officials with a wide range of positions and perspectives.

Our discussions with these officials were conducted both in person and by phone and included one to seven participants. Participants were asked a series of questions about their current congressional reporting and methods of tracking and reporting data:

- What security cooperation data does your office collect?
- What types of databases do you currently use to collect information?
- How is program funding tracked?
- How are program and financial data linked for reporting purposes?
- From your perspective, how might DoD's data gathering be improved?

---

[11] We interviewed more than 20 members of four CCMDs—U.S. Africa Command, U.S. Central Command, U.S. European Command, and U.S. Pacific Command—from the J3 (operations), J5 (planning), J4 (logistics), J8 (resources), and headquarters staff.

In an effort to benefit from the transparency efforts of other U.S. government agencies and organizations, our team reviewed the written reports on DoS's Foreign Assistance Data Review (FADR) process and USAID's *IATI Cost Management Plan* and held a series of discussions with DoS and USAID officials who have engaged in these initiatives to improve data collection and reporting on foreign aid.[12] These in-person and telephone discussions involved approximately 20 individuals in total and included members of the Foreign Aid Explorer and outside organizations that collect security cooperation data. We asked such questions as the following:

- How are foreign aid financial data tracked?
- Are data validated or vetted?
- What mechanisms have you developed to link program and financial data?
- To what extent has the working group process aided in the collection process?[13]

Research Limitations

Although we were still able to capture a wide range of perspectives of defense personnel across the security cooperation enterprise, we could obviously meet with only a small portion of the thousands of individuals who are engaged with security cooperation programs. Moreover,

---

[12] FADR was an effort DoS launched to better utilize its budget, financial, and program management systems to track and report on its foreign assistance programs for management purposes and to meet transparency and congressional reporting requirements. The *IATI Cost Management Plan* was an effort to outline a multiyear USAID effort to improve its reporting to IATI. See USAID, *International Aid Transparency Initiative (IATI) Cost Management Plan*, Washington, D.C., June 2015b; DoS, *Foreign Assistance Data Review Findings Report*, December 2015; and DoS, *Foreign Assistance Data Review: Phase Two—Data Element Index*, Winter 2016.

[13] It should be noted that all our focused discussions were not for attribution. RAND's Human Subjects Protection Committee reviewed our research and determined that it did not constitute human subjects research, meaning that it was designed solely to assess the performance of DoD programs.

due to funding limitations, we were unable to benefit from bringing these stakeholders together as a group to discuss the barriers they face in collecting data and the methods they have found to overcome these barriers. Such interactive discussions would have helped delineate the similarities and differences among programs and illuminate ways various offices might work together to improve security cooperation transparency in the future.

Another major limitation of our research was that, with the challenges of limited time and budget, we were able to analyze only a small number of security cooperation programs. Our selection of five security cooperation programs was intended to reflect the diversity security cooperation programs being reported to the Foreign Assistance Dashboard, but this set of five is not statistically representative of DoD's security cooperation programs. The number of programs and scope of reporting that DoD is required to provide are indeed much broader than what these programs can illustrate; indeed, it is a significant drawback that we cannot demonstrate the full complexity of the current reporting system or, likewise, provide the greater insight from a wider set of lessons-learned cases. The research reported here should be considered the first step toward gaining a more comprehensive picture of DoD's security cooperation reporting process and considering possible solutions to tracking data more effectively.

Organization of the Remainder of the Report

The organization of the report follows the order of our research. In Chapter Two, we present the results of our discussions with representatives from the Foreign Assistance Dashboard transparency organizations and our gap analysis to assess DoD's level of compliance with the dashboard, IATI, and PWYF ATI criteria. We offer recommendations for improving DoD reporting and raising its annually published transparency "ratings." We then discuss the implications of these foreign assistance transparency efforts for DoD's security cooperation reporting process more broadly.

In Chapter Three, we draw from our wide range of discussion with DoD personnel. We outline the major barriers DoD faces in collecting and reporting on security cooperation programs and then depict the process of security cooperation reporting for the five representative security cooperation programs. We analyze the comprehensiveness of congressional reporting requirements for each program, how well the program management and financial management communities were linked for data collection, the level and type of data collected, and the databases used to manage program and financial data for each. This serves to illustrate the complexity of the current system and to identify some of the workarounds that have been developed to overcome these barriers to meet existing reporting requirements.

Then, Chapter Four provides an overview of USAID's *IATI Cost Management Plan* and DoS's FADR effort and considers what best practices from these efforts to improve transparency for foreign aid reporting might apply to DoD's efforts to improve its process for collecting and reporting data on both foreign assistance and security cooperation programs.[14]

Finally, in Chapter Five, we summarize the results of our analysis and offer a number of short- and long-term recommendations for how DoD might improve compliance with IATI and begin to streamline the security cooperation reporting process to meet both new congressional reporting requirements and those DoD stakeholders might impose in the future.[15]

---

[14] USAID, 2015b; DoS, 2015.

[15] The companion document to this report provides more-detailed analysis of IATI's reporting criteria and DoD's process for meeting these requirements, as well as a more-complete mapping of the five security cooperation programs. The companion is available at http://www.rand.org/pubs/research_reports/RR2039.html.

CHAPTER TWO

The International Aid Transparency Initiative and What It Means for Security Cooperation Reporting Requirements

The U.S. decision to become a signatory to IATI in 2011 served as an important driver for transparency in security cooperation. While DoD was already providing data in a number of open forums, the commitment to IATI created new expectations for reporting specifically on foreign assistance activities in a common, standard format at an unprecedented level of detail. Moreover, it provided NGOs that promote transparency a means of rating DoD's compliance with these new standards for reporting. In this chapter, we explore the implications of the U.S. commitment to IATI by providing a brief description of the IATI organization and its standards for reporting on foreign assistance activities and an assessment of the degree to which DoD is currently meeting IATI standards and its associated ratings. From this assessment, we identify several potential areas for improving DoD's compliance with IATI standards and improving security cooperation transparency more broadly.

The United States Becomes a Signatory of IATI as Part of a Wider Transparency Effort

IATI is a voluntary effort organized by foreign aid donors, recipient countries, and civil society organizations aimed at making information on foreign aid spending easier to access, use, and understand. The initiative, which began in 2008, seeks to "to improve the transparency of aid, development, and humanitarian resources in order to increase their effectiveness in tackling poverty."[1] Signatories to the IATI agreement commit to publishing up-to-date foreign assistance data in an online registry using a common, standard format for reporting on the allocation of funds and the results of aid programs. The IATI registry has grown from its initial publication of data submissions from 12 of 18 signatories to posting data from 353 organizations based in 40 countries in 2015.[2]

The United States has engaged in the IATI process as an observer since 2008 and became a signatory to the initiative in 2011. Secretary of State Hillary Clinton announced the U.S. commitment to publishing data in the IATI registry at the High Level Forum on Aid Effectiveness in Busan, Korea, in November 2011, presenting the decision as part of an ongoing U.S. effort to encourage government transparency and accountability to increase the efficacy of U.S. foreign assistance and to increase international accountability for both donor and recipient nations.[3] This announcement followed the launch of the Foreign Assistance Dashboard in December 2010, which enabled users to track key foreign assistance budget and appropriation data for DoS and USAID, with a plan to include all agencies that provided assistance to foreign countries.[4] With its commitment to IATI, the United States went a step further in agreeing to provide data through the Foreign Assistance Dashboard to an international registry and to submit data according to common reporting standards. IATI's standards and the requirements for reporting to IATI through the Foreign Assistance Dashboard at ForeignAssistance.gov are described below.

---

[1] IATI, "About IATI," webpage, undated a.

[2] These organizations included the range of different kinds of NGOs, private sector and development finance institutions, and bilateral and multilateral Official Development Assistance providers and foundations as publishers. There appears to be a total of 13 donor countries reporting and 21 recipient partner countries. See IATI, *IATI Annual Report*, 2015.

[3] Tran, 2011.

[4] The dashboard was created as part of U.S. commitment to the Paris Declaration on Aid Effectiveness and the Accra Agenda for Action and in response to the open government initiative (Global Washington, "Foreign Assistance Dashboard—Bringing More Transparency to US Foreign Aid," Global WA website, December 23, 2010).

IATI Reporting Standards and Requirements

The key component of the initiative is the IATI Standard, which provides a technical framework for data submissions.[5] All organizations that provide foreign aid, including government donors, private-sector donors, private-sector organizations, and national and international NGOs, must comply with same standards in IATI's electronic format (which is in Extensible Markup Language [XML]) to link the IATI registry.[6] The IATI Standard has a total of 206 data elements; these are subdivided into the *IATI organization standard*, which includes 54 data elements describing the donor organization, and the *IATI activity standard*, which includes 152 data elements reporting the details of individual development cooperation activities or projects. Twelve of the 206 total data elements are mandatory—the minimum amount of data required for each activity recorded to the registry. These mandatory elements include three in the organization standard and nine in the activity standard. The mandatory elements include information on the donor organization (name, organization identifier, and identifier of the reporting organization) and on the activity (identifier, title, description, status, and start date).[7]

While IATI considers certain basic information on foreign aid activities and organizations to be mandatory—required for the organization to verify that data are presented in the proper format—it does not *require* organizations to provide any specific data elements or number or type of activities to the registry. According to IATI guidance, "the focus is very much on publishing what you can, based on what is readily available, ensuring [that] it is of reasonable quality, and also taking into account any exclusions. The idea is to then continu-

[5] IATI, undated a.

[6] IATI, undated a.

[7] The specific organization and mandatory elements for and sample data from the IATI database and all the specific data elements are included in a companion file (available at http://www.rand.org/pubs/research_reports/RR2039.html), as well as on IATI's website (IATI, homepage, undated c).

ally improve over time."[8] IATI encourages the publication of as much information as possible and is particularly interested in obtaining complete data on activities (particularly humanitarian assistance activities) and including forward-looking plans. The initiative does not assess participating organizations or countries based on the number of data elements they report. The IATI technical group evaluates the quality of all data submitted to the IATI registry to ensure that individual data sets are appropriately reported but does not assess the level of signatories' compliance. Thus, while the United States is committed to publishing as much detailed data as possible to the IATI registry according its organizational and activity standards, IATI does not grade it on the comprehensiveness of its reporting.

While IATI does not compare the data submitted across countries or agencies, certain NGOs do rate the relative levels of transparency on foreign aid. The PWYF organization, for example, extensively analyzes IATI data to produce its annual ATI. PWYF has its own methodology for scoring donor organizations, which includes 39 separate indicators across three categories—commitment to aid transparency, publishing organization-level data, and publishing activity-level data.[9] These indicators, which prioritize financial and performance information, do not directly correspond with the mandatory IATI standards. In 2012, PWYF gave DoD the lowest rating of any U.S. agency on the ATI index based on these criteria, receiving a "poor" score of 23 percent. In 2016, DoD improved to "fair," with a 46.7 percent score, yet still received the lowest rating of any U.S. agency.[10]

---

8 IATI, "IATI Standard: Guidance," webpage, undated d.

9 Each category is divided into subgroups and indicators and is weighted. It is important to note that the "commitment to aid transparency" category, which comprises 10 percent of the index score and consists of indicators on the quality of freedom of information legislation, implementation schedules, and database or portal accessibility, measures national-level phenomena within the U.S. government context and is outside DoD's direct control. DoD can directly affect 90 percent of its ATI score through the eight indicators on organization-level data, which is weighted at 25 percent, and the 28 indicators on activity-level data, which accounts for 65 percent of the overall score. See PWYF, "Aid Transparency Index: 2016 Index," 2016b.

10 PWYF, "Aid Transparency Index: 2016 U.S. Brief," 2016c, p. 4.

Foreign Assistance Dashboard Requirements

The requirements for U.S. government agencies to provide data for publication in the IATI registry are stipulated in OMB's Bulletin 12-01.[11] Bulletin 12-01 states that all U.S. government agencies must provide detailed budget, program, and financial information and data on their foreign assistance activities to the Foreign Assistance Dashboard.[12] The bulletin lists 22 government agencies that are required to submit data and specifically defines foreign assistance data as "tangible or intangible resources (goods, services, and/or funds) provided by the USG [U.S. government] to a foreign country," as authorized under the Foreign Assistance Act of 1961.[13] This definition goes beyond a strict definition of foreign aid for the purposes of development and thus includes aspects of U.S. security cooperation activities. DoD is, in fact, listed as one of the 22 agencies required to report data to the dashboard. It is important to note, however, that DoD, as a military organization, is unique among the organizations that are required to report to the Foreign Assistance Dashboard and that it is the only national defense agency currently reporting to IATI.[14]

---

[11] OMB, 2012.

[12] According to Bulletin 12-01 (OMB, 2012) guidance, data collected for the Foreign Assistance Dashboard should be used to meet multiple congressional reporting requirements, including USAID's annual report to Congress on U.S. foreign assistance, known as the "U.S. Overseas Loans and Grants" publication. (This publication, formerly known as the *USAID Greenbook*, is now available on online on USAID's Foreign Aid Explorer website.) Dashboard data are also expected to be used to prepare an annual report known as the "U.S. Official Development Assistance for the Development Assistance Committee of the Organization for Economic Co-operation and Development (OECD)," which is a requirement of committee membership.

[13] OMB, 2012, p. 4. The Foreign Assistance Act of 1961, as amended, states that assistance activities that are not explicitly authorized under the act but meet its definition of assistance are to be included to be consistent with historical collection and the spirit of transparency (OMB, 2012).

[14] The United Kingdom's Ministry of Defence is the only other defense organization to have published on IATI but has not done so since 2013. Thus, as an IATI representative reported, the U.S. DoD is a "trendsetter" in publishing foreign assistance activities to the registry and thus may be in a position to develop new standards for compliance by a military organization. Discussion with IATI representative, August 31, 2016.

DoS is the lead agency for implementing the Foreign Assistance Dashboard and is responsible for establishing a standardized framework for data reporting for the 22 agencies; collecting and submitting data to the dashboard; and posting the data, appropriately cross-walked to IATI standards, to the IATI registry.[15] According to Bulletin 12-01, DoS is not responsible for determining what data agencies provide or for validating data submissions, however. Each agency is "responsible for the accuracy and completeness of data provided." Moreover, each agency is "expected to improve its capacity to report the required information," once it begins submitting data to the dashboard.[16]

The dashboard's standardized reporting framework, which combines various U.S. foreign assistance reporting requirements, contained 189 possible data fields.[17] Of these, DoS required U.S. government agencies to focus reporting on 37 priority data fields, which include all 12 of IATI's mandatory elements, including the type of aid provided (e.g., program) and the obligation and disbursement figures for each activity.[18] As of 2016, a total of 55 data fields were reported on the Foreign Assistance Dashboard website. It should be noted that DoS's Office of Foreign Assistance Resources is seeking to increase all agencies' contributions to the Foreign Assistance Dashboard to include all 189 possible data fields, yet not all the data fields relevant to DoD's submissions.[19]

---

[15] This is conducted by DoS's Office of Foreign Assistance Resources.

[16] OMB, 2012, p. 8.

[17] The Foreign Assistance Dashboard established a list of 189 unique data fields, which correspond with 204 IATI fields that apply to the types of aid the U.S. government provides. While most U.S. agencies will not be able to report on all 189 (mainly because the fields do not apply to every agency's business processes), Foreign Assistance Dashboard managers plan over the long term to build capacity term to report as many of the 189 fields as possible. See ForeignAssistance.gov, "FA.gov Data Dictionary," June 27, 2017. Discussions with U.S. government officials, June 29, 2016.

[18] These 37 fields were selected to reflect the data elements that are common across the multiple foreign aid reporting requirements. Discussions with DoS and OSD practitioners, undated.

[19] Bulletin 12-01 (OMB, 2012) and focused discussions with U.S. government officials.

DoD's Submissions to the Foreign Assistance Dashboard

Our review of DoD data published to the Foreign Assistance Dashboard found that DoD published information in 40 of the Foreign Assistance Dashboard's 55 reported data fields. This extends beyond the dashboard's 37 priority fields to include such additional data as interagency transfer status, start and end dates, and planned start date.

We found that nearly all the data that DoD provided to these data fields were on the program or subprogram level, rather than the activity level. For CN, for example, there is only one listing per country per year, representing all activities and funding conducted under the International Counterdrug Program. Similarly, there is only one listing for each country for all the activities provided under the CTFP. In some cases, data are provided on a subprogram level, reflecting the program accounts from which the programs are funded. CTR is broken down into Cooperative Biological Engagement or Proliferation Prevention, for example, and the GT&E program includes individual funding accounts, such as Logistics Enhancement in a particular country. However, only the Humanitarian Civic Assistance program appeared to include activity level data (listing as many as 15 activities in the Philippines in one year), but this relatively small program covered only a limited number of countries and engagements.

We also noted that financial data were not reported consistently across DoD programs. Some programs included data on commitments, some on disbursements, and some on both. It was unclear what qualified as a commitment or disbursement for each program. Moreover, we found that some of the data reported to the Foreign Assistance Dashboard did not correspond with the data reported by or published in other DoD reports, such as in congressional budget justifications or Congressional Research Service reports, or on public websites, such as Foreign Aid Explorer, that purportedly drew on the same data sources. Some of these discrepancies can be explained in part by differences in how data are reported (Foreign Aid Explorer attributes security assistance to DoD, for example, while the Foreign Assistance Dashboard attributes it to DoS) and by differences in reporting time frame, but the mismatch in numbers reported to publicly accessible websites raises questions about data quality.[20]

RAND's Analysis of DoD's IATI Compliance

To better understand DoD's compliance with IATI requirements, we conducted a gap analysis to assess the extent to which DoD is reporting on the IATI Standard version 2.01 data elements and the 36 organization and activity-level indicators in PWYF's ATI.[21] We based our analysis on DoD's FY 2014 and FY 2015 submissions to the Foreign Assistance Dashboard.[22] As noted in Figure 2.1, we found that all 12 of IATI's minimum mandatory elements align with PWYF ATI indicators and Foreign Assistance Dashboard priority data fields. We found that 36 of the 39 PWYF ATI indicators align with elements that could be reported under IATI Standard Version 2.01. The three ATI indicators that are not included in the IATI Standard are the national-level indicators referenced earlier. We found that 17 priority data fields and six of the other data fields on the Foreign Assistance Dashboard are outside the scope of the IATI Standard elements and PWYF ATI indicators.

Overall, we found that DoD's reporting via the Foreign Assistance Dashboard overlaps with the majority of IATI's minimum mandatory elements and nearly one-half of the indicators in PWYF's index. It covers only a small portion of the total possible IATI elements, however. Specifically, we found the following:

- **DoD met most Foreign Assistance Dashboard priority requirements, some of which go beyond IATI.** DoD reports

[20] The discrepancies we found from a cursory comparison of data sources were discussed in GAO, *Foreign Assistance: Actions Needed to Improve Transparency and Quality of Data on ForeignAssistance.gov*, Washington, D.C., GAO-16-768, August 2016b.

[21] IATI, homepage, undated c; PWYF, 2016c.

[22] Recognizing the variation among the names and corresponding definitions giving to the elements, indicators, and data fields IATI, PWYF, and Foreign Assistance Dashboard use, we attempted to use our best judgment in comparing these components. Appendix C in the companion document (at http://www.rand.org/pubs/research_reports/RR2039.html) shows our work in piecing these components together.

Figure 2.1
Venn Diagram of Foreign Assistance Dashboard, IATI Standard, and PWYF ATI

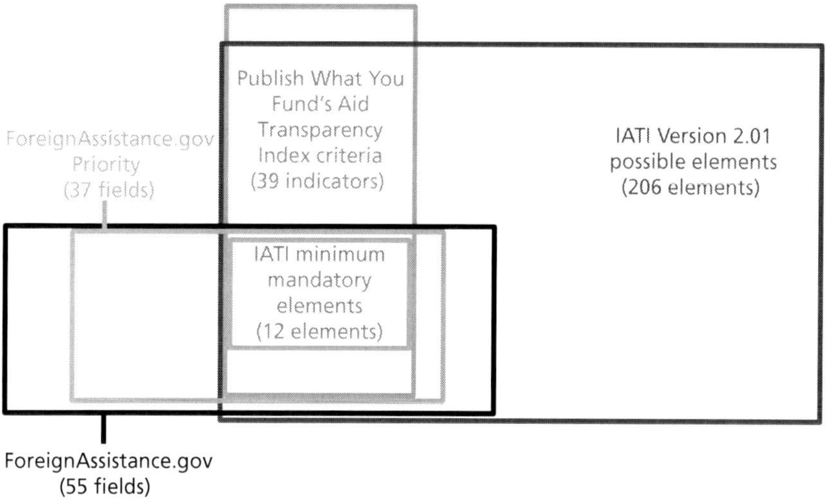

SOURCE: Foreign Assistance Dashboard, IATI Standard, and PWYF Aid Transparency Index.
RAND *RR2039-2.1*

on 28 of the 37 Foreign Assistance Dashboard data fields that its DoS managers have given priority. Seventeen of these fields are not included in the IATI Standard. DoD also reported on 11 fields through the Foreign Assistance Dashboard that are not deemed priority data fields, reporting primarily on program-level data for all these fields.

- **DoD met all 12 IATI minimum mandatory requirements and satisfied more than one-half of PWYF criteria.** DoD demonstrated compliance with 23 of 39 PWYF ATI indicators.[23] It did not meet two organizational-level and 13 activity-level PWYF ATI criteria, which included links to U.S. national strategy documents and allocation policy, memorandums of understanding

[23] We did not assess the three national-level PWYF ATI indicators described above because they fall beyond the scope of DoD's purview and reporting through the Foreign Assistance Dashboard.

with foreign partners, and budgetary information and impact assessment by activity.

- **DoD reports on the majority of the Foreign Assistance Dashboard's current data fields but only 20 percent of the total IATI elements.** DoD reports on 40 out of 55 fields in the dashboard but does not provide the detailed data on activities required to meet all 189 possible fields in the dashboard or the majority of elements in the IATI standards.

What DoD Can Do to Improve Its Compliance with IATI

One way to improve both DoD's PWYF ATI score and overall compliance with the IATI Standard is to **identify additional IATI elements that can be addressed**. We found that there are additional fields of data that it may be relatively easy for DoD to provide, such as adding links on the Foreign Assistance Dashboard to U.S. government websites that contain unclassified strategy documents and allocation policy documents. However, there are many elements DoD cannot include, such as tenders and contracts that apply only to development organizations, and such other elements as strategy documents, memoranda of understanding, or future plans, which are either classified or sensitive and whose release may jeopardize either U.S. relationships with other countries or the safety of U.S. forces and their foreign partners. One way that DoD can address these limitations is to **clarify what data elements or types of data can or cannot be released** to the public for national security reasons. The Foreign Assistance Dashboard provides for principled exceptions for data submissions that may be unclassified but could jeopardize U.S. personnel or recipients of U.S. resources or that could interfere with a U.S. agency effectively discharging its ongoing responsibilities. To effectively use this exemption, DoD will need to clearly and consistently define which categories of data qualify and to develop internal mechanism to vet data submissions to the Foreign Assistance Dashboard to ensure that no activities that meet this criteria are unintentionally submitted to the registry.

Additional clarification could distinguish between the types of security cooperation activities that qualify as foreign assistance and those that do not. IATI and PWYF encourage all agencies and governments to report as much as possible, so it is important for external audiences to have a clear understanding of which security cooperation programs or activities are conducted to gain information, access, or other operational benefits to U.S. forces and do not provide tangible or intangible benefits to a foreign partner. DoD will need to make as distinct a delineation as possible and to provide this definition consistently when submitting data to the Foreign Assistance Dashboard.

DoD could also **engage with representatives of the Foreign Assistance Dashboard** to learn which areas of foreign aid are particularly important to report. For instance, DoD could give a higher priority to reporting on humanitarian assistance activities, if the Foreign Assistance Dashboard representatives indicated that IATI were seeking to improve government reporting on such activities to encourage greater coordination of international humanitarian assistance efforts. This may not improve DoD's transparency ratings on completeness but could improve how the IATI community perceives DoD.

While DoD works most directly with DoS's Office of U.S. Foreign Assistance Resources to compile its reporting data, it might also be helpful to **engage with the IATI technical team** to clarify what data DoD can and cannot provide and to request tailored feedback and support on how to improve data reporting for unique programs or activities.[24] As the IATI Standard is still evolving, DoD's engagement with IATI may also prove helpful to adapting the technical framework in a way that could better accommodate reporting on foreign assistance that is outside the sphere of development aid. This may be of particular interest to IATI as improved DoD reporting may encourage other militaries to begin to report to the Registry.

DoD may also improve the quality of its reporting by **developing a mechanism to validate its submissions for completeness and accuracy**. It could adopt a simplified version of the "IATI Validator" tool that ensures that data are being submitted in the correct format.

---

[24] Discussion with IATI Technical Team representative, August 31, 2016.

The IATI tool checks publishers' files to ensure that they contain only valid XML inputs and elements defined in the relevant version of the IATI Standard and allows users to see how each publisher's data fares against these measures.[25] DoD could also check submissions against data reported by other sources, such as the Foreign Aid Explorer, annual reports to Congress, or congressional budget justification reports, to ensure that they are at least roughly aligned.[26]

To comply more fully with the IATI standards and make significant improvements in its ratings, DoD will need to expand the number of data fields reported on specific activities beyond the 37 priority fields Foreign Assistance Dashboard managers have requested. Such fields include disbursement information on individual activities and links to specific objectives, evaluations, and impact appraisals for each activity. However, providing this type of information would require a much higher level of detail in reporting and significant additional effort.

To date, nearly all the foreign assistance activity information that DoD has provided has been at the program or sector level. If DoD begins to report data at the activity level, the number of records that it reports will increase substantially. For example, our review of U.S. reporting to IATI revealed that, in FY 2014, DoD published 37 entries across five sample countries in the U.S. Pacific Command area of responsibility (AOR) and 15 entries across five sample countries in the U.S. European Command AOR. Yet, previous RAND research using G-TSCMIS data indicates that between 439 and 752 security cooperation–related activities were taking place in these countries at that time. Therefore, we would expect to see the number of activity-level entries to be at least 12 to 27 times those currently reported on the Foreign Assistance Dashboard.[27] This reaffirms that DoD was not providing

---

[25] IATI, "Dashboard," undated b.

[26] While other data sources capture somewhat different data and publish on different time lines, they can be used to ensure some consistency and guard against major errors.

[27] While not all security cooperation activities would qualify as foreign assistance, the number of activities recorded would undoubtedly be tens of times greater than currently reported (Jefferson P. Marquis, David E. Thaler, S. Rebecca Zimmerman, Megan Stewart, and Jeremy Boback, *The Global-Theater Security Cooperation Management Information System*

the level of detailed information required. Collecting, managing, and publishing detailed information on tens of thousands of DoD activities across the globe may prove to be insurmountable tasks for DoD for the immediate future, given the significant barriers DoD faces in security cooperation reporting. Chapter Three includes a discussion of the barriers for collecting more-detailed activity-level information.

Implications for Broader Security Cooperation Reporting

The challenges that DoD faces in providing greater transparency and detailed reporting on its foreign assistance activities to the Foreign Assistance Dashboard for publication to the IATI registry are indicative of the issues that DoD confronts in collecting and reporting on security cooperation data more broadly. IATI's focus on transparency in development aid requires DoD to clarify specifically what data for what programs qualify as foreign aid, yet the need to be clear and consistent in defining security cooperation and the limits to what can be reported on DoD's engagement activities applies not only to the Foreign Assistance Dashboard but also to a wider scope of DoD reporting requirements, including those in the FY 2017 NDAA. To ensure that DoD meets the intent of U.S. transparency initiatives and credibility among transparency advocates both inside and outside the government, DoD will need to clearly define when security cooperation meets the criterion of providing benefits to a foreign partner and when it is does not.

DoD's need to balance openly reporting data that benefits partner nations and the general public while safeguarding U.S. national security interests also applies beyond the Foreign Assistance Dashboard. The principled exceptions that apply to DoD submissions to the dashboard are relevant to all DoD activities, and the need to ensure that there is a mechanism for vetting potentially classified or sensitive data

Assessment and Implications for Strategic Users, Santa Monica, Calif.: RAND Corporation, 2016, Not available to the general public).

before allowing them to become public is a DoD-wide concern that must be applied to all external reporting.

Moreover, just as it needs to provide a system for validating the data that it posts to the Foreign Assistance Dashboard, DoD will need to develop a mechanism for fact-checking and reconciling all security cooperation data before they are reported externally. An initial step would be to compare data submissions with what is reported by the DoD Comptroller and USAID's Foreign Aid Explorer. This is not only critical to ensuring the accuracy of the data but also to ensuring that data are posted consistently across DoD and publicly in various published reports.

Finally, and most significantly, the expanding demand for data on foreign assistance and security cooperation funding more generally has presented DoD with a broader issue: The demand for data is overwhelming the current reporting process. The demand for security cooperation data within the U.S. government extends far beyond the demands for transparency from IATI or PWYF. DoD will undoubtedly need to commit a greater effort to collecting foreign assistance–related data and improving its process for reporting. This may require placing a greater initial effort on improving the quality of currently reported data before attempting to expand to additional fields. DoD may consider sacrificing potential short-term declines in transparency ratings to make more-substantial long-term improvements in transparency.

Moreover, given the potential for both increasing demands on the volume of data it reports and greater pressure from monitoring organizations, DoD will need to develop new mechanisms and processes to handle the exponentially increasing amounts of data it will need to report completely and accurately. An automated system for collecting and validating data to be submitted to the Foreign Assistance Dashboard would ensure better quality and consistency of data reporting as data requests increase on both foreign assistance and broader security cooperation activities. As introduced in Chapter One, improving compliance with IATI standards would not only help meet external demands but also begin to address some of the internal reporting challenges. In Chapter Three, we address some of the existing barriers to data collection and possible options for meeting both external and internal demands for greater transparency in reporting.

CHAPTER THREE

Challenges to Collecting Data on DoD Security Cooperation Programs and Ways to Overcome Them

Recent efforts to improve U.S. compliance with IATI standards reflect a broader challenge that DoD faces in reporting on security cooperation programs: Comprehensive data on the disbursement of funds for Title 10 (DoD) security cooperation activities are simply not available. While information on planned or obligated funding for certain security cooperation programs is tracked by country to meet current congressional reporting requirements, there is no overarching mechanism or process for tracking data on disbursements of funds by activity across all programs and no process for making this type of data readily accessible from existing program or financial databases and available for comprehensive assessment.

The G-TSCMIS software platform released in 2014 was designed to track the execution of security cooperation activities, rather than the disbursement of funds. Although the system includes a section or tab to document resources, users are not able to accurately collect or input information on final expenditures and are not able to draw on data from DoD financial systems. DoD officials report that, while G-TSCMIS has made significant advances over the past several years, the level of detail and complexity required to link this execution database with DoD accounting systems would overwhelm the current system.

This leaves DoD stakeholders without valuable data on security cooperation engagements to enable effective prioritization and resourcing decisionmaking. In this chapter, we provide an overview of the major barriers for collecting data on DoD security cooperation programs (as of 2016). We then map out five security cooperation programs that were reported to the Foreign Assistance Dashboard at that time to demonstrate how the complexity of the current system for planning, administering, and funding security cooperation programs has created barriers to comprehensive reporting. In doing so, we identify how some of the barriers for collecting data have been overcome to meet existing reporting requirements.

It is important to note that we refer here to security cooperation programs that were in place in 2016, prior to the implementation of the FY 2017 NDAA. Under the guidelines of the FY 2017 NDAA, many Title 10 security cooperation programs will be consolidated or expanded. The GT&E program (10 USC 2282) and some CN programs (Sections 1004 of P.L. 101-501 and 1033 of P.L. 105–85)[1] for example will be consolidated under a new authority, Section 333 of the 2017 NDAA (Public Law 114–328), "Foreign Security Forces: Authority to Build Capacity." Another program, the Developing Country Combined Exercise Program, will be expanded, under the new Section 321 of the 2017 NDAA, "Training with friendly foreign countries: payment of training and exercise expenses."[2] The implications of these changes were not known at the time of this writing; however, it is likely that many of the current barriers to security cooperation reporting will remain.

Current Barriers to Security Cooperation Reporting

Before any improvements in reporting can be made, it important to understand why it is so difficult for DoD to gather comprehensive data on its security cooperation programs. It is not simply that there is no

---

[1] DoD's authority to engage with foreign partners to combat drug trafficking was derived from statutes in Public Law that were subsequently reauthorized and expanded but not codified into U.S. Code. These authorities include P.L. 101-501, §1004, "Support for Counter-Drug Activities," and P.L. 105–85, §1033, "Authority to Provide Additional Support for Counter-Drug Activities of Other Countries," which was reauthorized in 2014.

[2] FY 2017 NDAA (P.L. 114–328).

system in place to collect information across programs but that the nature of DoD's engagements with its foreign partners and the way in which security cooperation programs have evolved since 2001 have made the tracking and reporting of DoD activities extraordinarily difficult. The processes that have been developed for planning, executing, and funding security cooperation programs also create significant obstacles to sharing common data across offices. Moreover, DoD's complex accounting systems create inherent impediments to capturing end-to-end financial data for activities that extend across multiple countries, layers of command, agencies, and years. These barriers are outlined in greater detail below.

Security Cooperation Programs Are Based on a Patchwork of Authorities

Tracking and reconciling financial data is a common problem throughout DoD; however, it is particularly problematic for security cooperation programs, which are derived from a multitude of legislative authorities.[3] In a 2016 study, RAND identified 123 Title 10 statutes that authorize the Secretary of Defense to cooperate with foreign partners.[4] These statutes were enacted over several decades, most since the terrorist attacks of September 11, 2001, to meet various U.S. national security requirements. As a result, security cooperation programs have a range of objectives and operational components, from providing

---

[3] DoD's decentralized environment and hundreds of nonstandard financial management business processes and systems have made it difficult for the agency to meet reporting requirements for decades. Since 1997, DoD has been unable to meet a congressional requirement to prepare audited financial statements. The FY 2010 NDAA (P.L. 111-84) mandated that DoD develop and maintain a plan that describes the actions needed to ensure that its consolidated financial statements are audit ready by September 30, 2017. While DoD has made significant progress in implementing the Financial Improvement and Audit Readiness (FIAR) guidance, the GAO has indicated that the process has not yet resulted in a fundamental transformation of systems and operations necessary to resolve the department's long-standing financial management deficiencies. See GAO, *High-Risk Series: Progress on Many High-Risk Areas, While Substantial Efforts Needed on Others*, Washington, D.C., GAO-17-317, February 2017, and GAO, *DoD Financial Management: Greater Visibility Needed to Better Assess Audit Readiness for Property, Plant, and Equipment*, Washington, D.C., GAO-16-383, May 2016a.

[4] Thaler et al., 2016.

disaster assistance to providing direct operational support to counterdrug missions. These programs draw from a variety of sources of funding, from DoD's operations and maintenance account and direct congressional appropriations and, in some cases, from both.[5] The programs maintain different management structures, with some managed by OSD, some by DSCA, and some by DTRA. They provide various roles and responsibilities to the CCMDs for managing activities and resources and involve numerous military departments and agencies, and often contractors, in partner-nation engagements. As a result, the programs have different limitations and constraints on what can and cannot be reported. The diversity of authorities is evident across the five security cooperation programs that we map later in this chapter. As will be noted, mixed funding streams from multiple security cooperation funding accounts have been a major obstacle to tracking and reporting on spending.[6]

Planning, Program, and Financial Communities Operate Separately

The complexity of the administration of security cooperation programs poses a second major barrier to data collection. Each program requires the engagement of DoD policy, planning, program management, and financial management offices at various levels of operation. Yet each of these communities has different perspectives, different data requirements, and limited opportunities or needs to share data. Security cooperation planners, for example, focus on strategic planning and the development of project proposals, and program managers concentrate on project execution. The information that they collect varies accordingly. Planners maintain data on proposed projects, while program managers track projects that have been approved and executed. Financial managers are further separated; they collect data on financial transactions that are reported separately for accounting purposes.

---

[5] Funding for some security cooperation authorities is subsumed under a larger budget category or simply drawn from the overall DoD operations and maintenance budget, making identification of funding levels particularly difficult.

[6] DoD officials across OSD, DSCA, and the CCMDs cited mixed funding streams and multiple funding accounts for programs as obstacles to tracking spending. Discussions with DoD officials, June 3, 2016; June 17, 2017; and June 29, 2016.

Moreover, the systems used for recording data differ, making it difficult to combine or compare information across offices or communities. The CCMDs use their own systems for strategic planning, such as the Integrated U.S. Africa Command Theater Synchronization System, which operate separately from systems designed for submitting proposals, such as the Overseas Humanitarian Assistance Shared Information System—and both operate separately from G-TSCMIS, which is designed to track the execution of security cooperation activities. The comptroller records financial information on disbursements on separate accounting systems that are often divorced from program reporting. (It is important to note that, while estimated financial data are included in the planning and budgeting process, program managers do not have direct access to data on the actual disbursement of funds.) Table 3.1 illustrates the divisions between the communities. As we will discuss in more detail later, program systems of record and financial systems of record not only collect different types of information but lack common data fields or ways to link programmatic and financial data.

Financial Data Are Not Consistently Defined, Tracked, or Reported

A fundamental challenge with security cooperation reporting is that financial data are not consistently reported across programs. Programs report different types of financial data depending on their reporting requirements and data availability. Some security cooperation programs report commitments; some report obligations; some report disbursements; and yet others report planned spending. Adding to the complexity, similar financial terms are used at different levels or stages of accounting.

Commitments occur when the U.S. government sets aside, or reserves, funds for a specific purpose. Obligations are the financial transactions associated with commitments that require, or obligate, the U.S. government to make a payment by some designated time. Once a transaction associated with the commitment is processed, an obligation is incurred.[7] Disbursed funds (also referred to as *outlays*) are

---

[7] The Foreign Assistance Dashboard defines obligated funds as those that "have been applied to activities and are referred to as obligations because they obligate the Federal Gov-

Table 3.1
Stovepiping of Security Cooperation Planning, Program, and Financial Communities in DoD

	Stovepiped Systems		
	Policy and Planning	**Program Management**	**Financial Management**
Reporting requirements	Notifications on proposals	Annual or biannual reports on program obligations or expenditures	Congressional budget justifications
Communities	OSD, DSCA CCMD J5, Strategic Planning and Policy Security cooperation officer (SCO)	DSCA, DTRA CCMD J3, Operations; J4, Logistics; J5, Strategic Planning and Policy Implementing agencies SCO	Comptrollers CCMD J8, Resources and Assessment Services' budget offices Contracting agencies
Data collected	Project proposals or planned spending	Projects planned, estimated costs, allocations	DoD-wide transactions DSCA obligations Service obligations Contractor receipts
Data and systems	Proposal databases CCMD strategic planning	Program management databases Execution database (G-TSCMIS) Excel spreadsheets	DoD systems (DFAS) Service systems Contracting agency systems

SOURCES: Discussions with DoD officials.

those expended by the government to pay, or liquidate, its obligations.[8] However, these terms are often used in reference to different stages of

ernment to make outlays either immediately or in the future. Obligations may include a range of transactions, e.g., contracts, grants, guarantees, assistance agreements, etc." (Foreign Assistance Dashboard, webpage, undated). DoD 7000.14-R, *Department of Defense Financial Management Regulation*, various dates, p. G-22, defines an obligation as an "[a]mount representing orders placed, contracts awarded, services received, and similar transactions during an accounting period that will require payment during the same, or a future, period."

8 Foreign Assistance Dashboard, webpage, undated; DoD 7000.14, pp. G-14 and G-23.

the accounting process. According to DoD officials, there is no clear consensus on when commitments formally occur during the process of allocating security cooperation funds.[9] This ambiguity extends to obligations and disbursements as well; the determination of what "counts" as an obligation or disbursement can vary by program and level of activity. For example, the OSD Comptroller may consider funds allocated to DSCA for OHDACA as an obligation; DSCA may consider the allocation of funds to a CCMD for humanitarian activities to be an obligation; and the CCMD may not consider the funds to be obligated until they have been allocated to implementing agencies to conduct a particular activity, at which point funds go into regular accounting systems for execution. Because financial transactions occur at multiple levels, the OSD Comptroller and DSCA must pick one position to report.[10] However, it is often unclear which position is being reported.

Tracking of financial data also suffers from visibility problems because of multiple systems with limited interoperability. Each military department has its own accounting system, which makes it hard to follow the transfer of funds both to and from the CCMDs. The CCMDs use their executive agent's system of record, yet components within the CCMDs use their respective services' accounting systems.[11] U.S. European Command, for example, uses the Army's General Fund Enterprise Business System as its financial system, while forces conducting security cooperation activities in Europe under U.S. Naval Forces Europe use the Navy's Enterprise Resource Planning system, and U.S. Air Forces in Europe uses a third accounting system. Moreover, the systems use different codes and fund identifiers, making it difficult to follow funding through to execution. This is illustrated in more detail later, in the "Five Security Cooperation Programs" section.

[9] Discussions with U.S. defense officials, August 2016.

[10] Discussions with U.S. defense officials, October 21, 2016.

[11] Each geographic CCMD has its own executive agent. The U.S. Air Force is the executive agent for U.S. Central Command; the U.S. Navy is the executive agent U.S. Pacific Command; and the U.S. Army is the executive agent for U.S. European Command, U.S. Africa Command, U.S. Southern Command, and U.S. Northern Command. Discussions with U.S. DoD officials June 17, 2016, and October 5, 2016.

Reported Data Are Rarely Reconciled or Verified

Another obstacle to collecting consistent information on security cooperation programs is that reported data are rarely reconciled or verified, despite varying time lines for the obligation and disbursement of funds and differences across offices in the way information is reported. While most security cooperation programs have one to two years to obligate funds after Congress allocates them, expenditure of funds may occur up to five years after obligation, during "expired" years. Annual reporting requirements often do not allow for the reconciliation of funding from previous years and may therefore not consistently capture security cooperation spending.[12]

Financial data reported by different offices inside and outside DoD also vary significantly because of the different time lines for collecting data and the different criteria for defining security cooperation activities. Funding reported in the Foreign Military Training Report (FMTR) differs from information in the annual reports to Congress, the DSCA Historical Facts Book, and the Foreign Assistance Dashboard.[13] Notable variations can also be found in data the DoD comptroller provides the congressional budget justification reports or in data from other entities, such as GAO, Congressional Research Service, and USAID's Foreign Aid Explorer (formerly known as the *USAID Greenbook*), that obtain information directly from DoD. (To cite one example, the total amount of spending for OHDACA in 2014 was reported as $6,800,499 on the Foreign Assistance Dashboard, $134,346,383 on Foreign Aid Explorer, and $163,591,000 in actual spending in DSCA's FY 2016 budget estimate.[14]) Currently, there is no mechanism for reconciling or verifying much of this data before they are released to the public. Similarly, there is no comprehensive process for vetting security

[12] Discussions with U.S. defense officials, August 10, 2016.

[13] U.S. Department of Defense and U.S. Department of State Joint Report to Congress, *Foreign Military Training and DoD Engagement Activities of Interest* (FMTR), Washington, D.C., 2016; DSCA, *Historical Facts Book: Foreign Military Sales, Foreign Military Construction Sales and Other Security Cooperation Historical Facts*, Washington, D.C., September 30, 2015b.

[14] Foreign Assitance.gov, undated; USAID, undated; and DSCA, "Fiscal Year 2016 Budget Estimates: Overseas Humanitarian, Disaster, and Civic Aid," February 2015a.

cooperation data to confirm that the information is not classified or sensitive to ensure that its public disclosure does not negatively affect U.S. national security interests.

Five Security Cooperation Programs Demonstrate the Barriers to Reporting and Workarounds

To depict how barriers for collecting security cooperation data have been overcome to meet existing reporting requirements, we mapped out the process for data collection for five security cooperation programs: OHDACA, GT&E, CN, CTFP, and CTR. Our sponsor selected these five programs to reflect a cross section of the 13 DoD programs that were reported to the Foreign Assistance Dashboard in FY 2016. Each has different congressional reporting requirements, sources of funding, and management structures.[15] For one program, requirements were limited to reporting only on the total amount of funds obligated each year or notifying Congress on the commencement of activities; for another, program managers are required to provide a detailed accounting of obligations and expenditures on each activity and a description of all the agencies and contractors engaged to carrying out the activity. Sources of funding vary, from DoD's operations and maintenance account to direct congressional appropriations. One program has a central funding account, while the others do not. Some of the programs are managed by DSCA through various offices; one is managed by OSD and one by DTRA. These five programs depict much of the diversity that exists across security cooperation programs more broadly, although they clearly do not represent a statistically significant sample of all 176 security cooperation programs that were in effect at the time.

We next provide a brief overview of the five programs, a summary of congressional reporting requirements, and a depiction of the challenges in meeting both these requirements and those of the Foreign

[15] At the start of this research in FY 2016, a total of 13 DoD programs were being reported to the Foreign Assistance Dashboard. In FY 2017, 24 programs were being reported.

Assistance Dashboard. We conclude with a summary of the best practices that may be drawn from each of the programs.[16]

Overseas Humanitarian Disaster and Civic Aid

OHDACA, which is often referred to as if it were a single program, actually consists of five separate Title 10 authorities that relate to humanitarian assistance. The five statutes provide DoD with the authority to transport humanitarian material and material for NGOs, donate excess supplies, conduct humanitarian mine action programs, and provide foreign disaster relief.[17] While the OHDACA authorities are linked by a common funding appropriation, they each maintain separate legislative restrictions and reporting requirements.[18] Annual reporting requirements vary in their specificity but do not extend beyond an accounting of the total obligation of funds by program. None of the authorities requires information on the obligation of funds by country

[16] The companion document to this report describes the mapping exercise and provides details of the reporting process for each of the five programs. The companion is available at http://www.rand.org/pubs/research_reports/RR2039.html.

[17] The OHDACA account, established by the FY 1995 NDAA (P.L. 103-337), Section 1411, included six humanitarian assistance-related authorities. They include authorities for the transport of humanitarian material (10 USC 2561 and 10 USC 402), the donation of excess nonlethal supplies (Section 2557), humanitarian mine action programs (10 USC 407), and foreign disaster relief (10 USC 404). One more section, 10 USC 401, authorizes humanitarian and civic assistance activities in conjunction with military operations; while this program is part of OHDACA, it is managed separately from the other five DoD humanitarian assistance programs and is therefore reported independently. Since 2011, it has been managed by the Joint Staff. See Nina Serafino, *The Department of Defense Role in Foreign Assistance: Background, Major Issues, and Options for Congress*, Washington, D.C.: Congressional Research Service, RL34639, December 9, 2008; DSCA, "Humanitarian Assistance, Disaster Relief and Mine Action," information paper, Washington, D.C., July 2012; DSCA, *Fiscal Year 2017 President's Budget Defense Security Cooperation Agency (DSCA): Overseas Humanitarian, Disaster, and Civic Aid*, Washington, D.C., February 2016b; and GAO, *Humanitarian Development Assistance: Project Evaluation and Better Information Sharing Needed to Manage Military's Efforts*, Washington, D.C., February 2012.

[18] For example, 10 USC 2561 requires an annual report on the total amount of funds obligated for humanitarian relief and the number of completed transportation missions. On the other hand, 10 USC 404 requires notifying Congress after the commencement of disaster assistance activities. See DSCA, *Security Assistance Management Manual*, Washington, D.C., 2017.

at the level of detail the Foreign Assistance Dashboard requires, which includes funding disbursements by country and activity.[19]

The DSCA Program Management office, which maintains programmatic oversight of all OHDACA-funded activities, is responsible for meeting most congressional reporting requirements and submitting data to the Foreign Assistance dashboard. It faces a number of barriers for collecting and reporting information. The fact that it is responsible for reporting on five humanitarian assistance programs with different requirements adds to the complexity of the task. A lack of visibility on the execution of humanitarian activities is also a major limiting factor. While DSCA and OSD's Special Operations and Low Intensity Conflict (SO/LIC) office are involved in the project proposal and notification process for OHDACA programs, the CCMDs are responsible for determining when and how humanitarian assistance activities are executed; this information is not easily accessible to DSCA program managers. As CCMDs often hold on to humanitarian assistance funding until the end of the FY (to ensure that funding is available to meet unexpected needs), there can also be a lag in the availability of data.[20] Moreover, because most OHDACA funding is allocated to the CCMD, rather than to specific countries, information on activities in a particular country is often difficult to come by.

Other barriers include the fact that program data on OHDACA are collected on the Overseas Humanitarian Assistance Shared Information System (OHASIS) and G-TSCMIS, yet neither system includes information on the disbursement of funds. Although OHASIS and G-TSCMIS include resource tabs, they are not connected to authoritative financial data sources. Thus, these tabs rely on data that are manually input by planners, typically include only estimated spending, and are not reliably populated. DoD officials note that OHASIS

---

[19] At the time of this writing, it does not appear that the OHDACA program will be consolidated with any other programs. The FY 2017 NDAA (P.L. 114–328) does, however, authorize monitoring and evaluation of overseas humanitarian, disaster, and civic aid programs of DoD (OHDACA is referred in a separate section of the 2017 NDAA, Sec. 1272, "Monitoring and evaluation of overseas humanitarian, disaster, and civic aid programs of the Department of Defense.")

[20] Discussion with DoD officials, June and September 2016.

includes only estimated costs used during the project proposal process and that G-TSCMIS is used for coordinating the execution of activities.[21] Financial information on OHDACA is collected separately by the DSCA comptroller's office, which also faces obstacles to tracking the distribution of funds to the country or activity level: Funds are provided to the CCMDs as two-year obligations, which are then allocated to implementing agencies that have up to five years to spend the money. With each fund transfer, the comptroller's visibility becomes more limited as money is transferred into different accounting systems; thus, determining the annual expenditures of funds becomes increasingly difficult over the course of a five-year spending cycle.[22] The integration of financial data with program data presents additional challenges; program managers often have no access to the financial management systems, and there are few standardized coding systems across offices to track funding by country.

To meet existing annual reporting requirements on the obligations of funds by program for OHDACA authorities, DSCA program and financial managers have adopted a number of workarounds. Requirements for reporting on the total obligations and number of missions conducted each year are met by drawing on data in OHASIS on planned activities and conferring with the CCMDs. Financial managers rely on estimated dollar values for each program authority and report their allocations to the CCMDs as obligations.[23] To obtain more-comprehensive information on country-level activities, DSCA managers engage program officers at the CCMD level and SCOs in particular countries, who often maintain data on individual spreadsheets.[24] This more arduous process of contacting defense personnel at

---

[21] Estimated costs are generally provided by the SCOs, components, or contracting agencies that implement activities. Discussion with DoD officials, June 17, 2016

[22] The level of visibility also varies by type of transfer, with some types (such as Military Interdepartmental Purchase Requests [MIPRs]) being harder to track than others. Discussion with DoD officials, June and September 2016.

[23] Discussion with DoD officials, June and September 2016.

[24] SCOs are also referred to as *offices of defense cooperation*.

the country level is necessary to obtain more detailed data for the Foreign Assistance Dashboard.

A best practice adopted by the OHDACA program is the use of the OHASIS system to integrate information on project proposals across policy and program management offices, as well as the CCMDs. While it does not include information on disbursements, data on allocations are tracked more carefully as a result.

Global Train and Equip

The GT&E program was established under Section 1206 of the FY 2006 NDAA (P.L. 109-163) to provide DoD with special authority to rapidly train and equip foreign military partners for CT and stability operations. The program was later expanded to include the authority to build the capacity of a foreign country's maritime, border security, or other national-level security forces, when it was codified under 10 USC 2282 in 2015.[25]

Congress imposed a number of unique reporting rules on the GT&E program, including requirements to notify Congress within 15 days of all proposed activities and to provide an annual assessment of the operational capacity and performance of the GT&E recipients. According to DoD officials, these congressional notifications constitute financial commitments.[26] These requirements do not include reporting on the disbursement of funding for GT&E activities by country, yet DoD faces a number of obstacles to meeting both current and Foreign Assistance Dashboard requirements.[27]

---

[25] The FY 2017 NDAA (P.L. 114–328) repeals 10 USC 2282 and replaces it with 10 USC 333, which consolidates several existing authorities. It expands the purposes of activities to including counterterrorism, counter–weapons of mass destruction (WMD), counterdrug, counter–transnational organized crime, maritime and border security, military intelligence, humanitarian assistance, national interest operations and foreign national territory defense. See Security Assistance Monitor, "Defense Bill Breakdown: Key Military Aid Issues in the FY 2017 National Defense Authorization Act, September 26, 2016.

[26] Discussions with U.S. defense officials, August 8 and August 26, 2016.

[27] CCMD submits 10 USC 2282 proposals to OSD (SO/LIC) to specify requirements. DSCA oversees a feasibility review of the proposals to identify procurement and other issues with CCMD equipment lists and training requirements, which serve as the memorandum

Although OSD's SO/LIC office is responsible for providing notifications to Congress on GT&E proposals and for submitting annual assessments of particular 10 USC 2282 programs, DSCA is responsible for determining the costs of GT&E proposals and managing the acquisition and delivery of equipment and training to partner nations and is therefore responsible for compiling the data required for reporting purposes. DSCA's Security Assistance and Equipping Directorate faces many of the same obstacles the OHDACA program officer encounters in accessing information from the CCMDs and gaining visibility on the execution of train and equip activities. Program and financial management information on train and equip activities are also collected via separate processes on different systems: the Defense Security Assistance Management System (DSAMS) for equipment, Security Assistance Network Web Tool (SANWeb) for training, and the Defense Finance and Accounting Service (DFAS) for finances. Moreover, because the 10 USC Section 2282 authority does not require reporting on the disbursement of funds, most of the data DSCA collects are focused on the proposal process, which rests at the CCMD level rather than the country level.[28]

Still, DSCA's Security Assistance and Equipping Directorate has been able to collect detailed data on acquisition and delivery of equipment through the adoption of a pseudo-FMS process, in which equipment that is purchased by the U.S. government is administered as if it had been sold directly to a partner nation. Similar to FMS, a DoD implementing agency develops a letter of offer and acceptance in DSAMS for each GT&E case. Although this "pseudo" letter of offer and acceptance is not signed by the partner nation, it serves to document the transfer of articles and services and enables DSCA to ensure that every equipment delivery is completed by the end of the

of request to the implementing agency. The proposals are simultaneously reviewed and prioritized by OSD (SO/LIC), the Joint Staff, and DoS; approved by the Secretary of Defense; and then submitted for congressional notification

[28] DSCA and SO/LIC are only required to submit annual reports that include an assessment of the operational capacity and performance of the recipient units.

year, returned, or reconciled.[29] It also allows the DSCA comptroller to track data on allocations, amounts reallocated, unobligated balances, and unliquidated obligations. In addition, it makes information on equipment-related GT&E cases accessible to program officers within the CCMDs and SCOs through the publicly accessible Security Cooperation Information Portal (SCIP),[30] thus providing a means of linking different DoD communities.[31]

Interestingly, GT&E funds that move through the pseudo-FMS case process are easier to reconcile as cases are modified to reflect changes to funding.[32] If for some reason the funds are not expended during the expired years or are shifted to another case, unliquidated obligations or deobligated funds are captured in the case reconciliation process. However, these changes may not be captured in reports on activities or obligations that were already published, potentially contributing to conflicting numbers.

The pseudo-FMS process does not provide a means of validating data, however. According to DoD officials, the quality of the data that are input into SCIP is inconsistent, both for FMS and pseudo-FMS cases.[33] Program managers in the CCMDs often develop their own

[29] The pseudo–letter of offer and acceptance is also helpful for end-use monitoring for equipment. Tracking of training is less comprehensive.

[30] DSCA, "Security Cooperation Information Portal: SCIP Background," January 2016a.

[31] SCIP was designed to allow international customers and U.S. government personnel to view information on FMS cases managed across different military departments. It uses a search engine to pull in data from DSAMS, the Defense Integrated Financial System, Centralized Information System for International Logistics, Management Information System for International Logistics, the Security Assistance Management Information System, the Enhanced Freight Tracking System, and end-use monitoring. The Security Cooperation Management Suite is a joint service, web-based capability within SCIP that provides U.S. government personnel with end-to-end visibility of the FMS case process. It draws from DSAMS, financial accounting systems, and external data systems. It permits manual data entry and data sharing of information that is not available through an automated source. Training data, which are not on the SCIP portal, are not captured as comprehensively as equipment.

[32] Discussions with DSCA, October and November 2016.

[33] While some defense officials described the data quality as inconsistent, the data do provide a means of sharing information on specific activities. Phone discussion with defense

informal workarounds to ensure that the data that appear in the system are correct, contacting the component that executed the case or calling the DSCA country director or an individual SCO to determine the status of the equipment and training delivered to a particular country within their AOR.

Counternarcotics

DoD's engagement in CN activities is derived from four statutes in Public Law that provide the U.S. military with the authority to engage with foreign forces to combat drug trafficking. These statues provide DoD with the authority to train foreign police forces to engage in counterdrug activities; provide nonlethal equipment to certain countries; support Colombia's unified counterdrug and CT campaign; and engage a task force to support law enforcement agencies conducting CN, CT, and counter–transnational organized crime missions.[34] Reflecting the confusing patchwork of authorities, DoD's CN activities are often covered by more than one of these laws, which retain distinct legal and operational requirements.[35]

The four CN authorities are linked by a common funding mechanism and reporting requirement, however. All DoD drug interdiction and counterdrug activities are funded through a single DoD Central Transfer Account and are required to be reported to Congress on a biannual basis through what is known as a 1009 report.[36] This 1009 report must provide Congress with the total amount of CN assistance

---

officials, October 6, 2016.

[34] DoD CN authorities have not been codified into U.S. Code but have been reauthorized and expanded through congressional legislation since the 1990s. For more detail on these authorities, see Thaler et al., 2016.

[35] The FY 2017 NDAA (P.L. 114–328) separates the U.S. counterdrug authorities between activities that provide counterdrug or counter–transnational organized crime support to other U.S. government bodies and U.S. police forces in support of foreign law enforcement and activities that build the capacity of foreign forces, which fall under the new multipurpose "train and equip" authority. The implications of these new authorities were not clear at the time of this writing.

[36] Section 1009 refers to Section 1009 of the FY 2013 NDAA (P.L. 112-239), as amended through subsequent congressional authorizations.

provided by country, a description of the types of counterdrug activities conducted, and the legal authority under which this assistance was provided.[37] The report is not required to include data on disbursements by activity. It stipulates that DoD provide information only on the "expenditure of funds by project code," meaning the obligation of funds for general categories of CN activities.

CN programs have more extensive reporting requirements than OHDACA and GT&E programs, as well as a number of unique barriers to collecting information on security cooperation activities. First, because CN laws authorize DoD to engage in both direct and indirect counterdrug missions, some DoD activities operational or are intended to gather information for U.S. purposes and provide little or no benefit to a partner nation and, therefore, would not qualify as foreign assistance. Second, in some cases, U.S. activities may take place in one country for the benefit of another. (A regional CN conference held in Hong Kong, for example, might be recorded as taking place in China but would also benefit participants from nearby countries.) This makes it difficult to classify certain counterdrug activities as strictly security cooperation or foreign assistance, or to determine what countries should be considered the recipient of U.S. aid.

The Office of the Deputy Assistant Secretary of Defense (DASD) for Counternarcotics and Global Threats (CN&GT), which is responsible for both providing program oversight and collecting data for reports, also faces difficulty tracking detailed, country-level data through the CN Central Transfer Account. Funds transferred from the that account to the CCMDs, services, and DoD agencies flow through more than 20 different accounts. The CN funds are designated for a particular purpose or intended effect, rather than for a specific country or activity. As a result, the CN&GT office has little visibility into where or how CN funds are ultimately used, which creates a third major barrier for collecting country-level information.

To capture the data necessary to meet its congressional reporting requirements, the CN&GT office developed its own web-based database, where DoD services and components provide quarterly obli-

---

[37] Section 1009, P.L. 112-239, as amended

gation reports on CN activities. The database tracks general types of CN activities (as required by Congress) by assigning project codes to all recorded obligations. These project codes are maintained within the accounting systems of each CCMD, service, and agency that receives CN funding. Implementing agencies are also required to include information on the legal authority under which each of these general categories of activities were conducted and the country in which they occurred on the database. Data are input manually, although the compilation of data requires the coordinated efforts of program management and financial offices. Information in the database is also validated to some degree by a voluntary audit of the each year by the DoD Inspector General's office.[38]

While the CN database and Inspector General's report serve as effective workarounds for gathering data across services and agencies on a quarterly basis and meeting the requirement for the 1009 report, they do not provide the level of detailed information required for the Foreign Assistance Dashboard. The database captures the obligation of funds rather than disbursements, and CN project codes fail to provide sufficient granularity because they are used to designate a particular purpose or intended effect, rather than a particular country or activity. This level of detail is particularly difficult for the CN&GT office to provide because the CN&GT office is outside the Joint Staff command structure and is not managed by DSCA. The office thus cannot contact SCOs directly to obtain clarification on CN activities when needed, as other program managers operating out of the CCMDs or DSCA are able to do.

Combating Terrorism Fellowship Program

The Regional Defense CTFP was established in 2002 to fund targeted CT educational and training programs for foreign military officers and

---

[38] Discussions with DoD officials, August 2016, and U.S. Department of Defense, Inspector General, *Independent Auditor's Report on the FY 2015 DoD Detailed Accounting Report for the Funds Obligated for National Drug Control Program Activities*, Alexandria, Va., DODIG-2016-041 January 29, 2016.

security officials. The program, which was codified by 10 USC 2249c,[39] provides DoD with the authority to pay the costs for mid- to senior-level personnel to attend educational institutions, conferences, and training programs inside and outside the United States.[40]

The reporting requirements outlined in 10 USC 2249c are comprehensive. Annual reports to Congress are required to include a complete accounting of program expenditures by country and the total number of students trained and lists of every training course the foreign officers attend. The annual report must also provide an assessment of the effectiveness of the CTFP in meeting U.S. CT objectives and include a justification of how the program fits within the theater security priorities.

DSCA's Directorate of Building Partnership Capacity, which manages the CTFP and is responsible for producing the CTFP annual report, faces a number of obstacles to collecting such comprehensive data. Like the GT&E program office, it relies on SANWeb to track information on the training of foreign military and security officials and faces many of the same obstacles to ensuring that all training data are input into the system and validated. Funding information is also difficult to follow on SANWeb because most data entered into the system relate to estimated costs or obligations, rather than to disbursements, and are not linked to DSCA's financial management system.

Over the course of the past several years, the CTFP program has adopted a number of workarounds to overcome these obstacles by creating a specialized coding structure for program activities within the SANWeb and engaging CTFP managers at the CCMDs to facilitate the data-gathering process. CTFP data on the SANWeb are identified by a country code, implementing agency code and FY and program type.[41] The Directorate of Building Partnership Capacity also coordinates with the DSCA comptroller on a quarterly basis to reconcile

---

[39] Subsequently renumbered to be 10 USC 345.

[40] The FY 2017 NDAA (P.L. 114–328) consolidates authority for the CTFP with other security cooperation programs under 10 USC Ch. 16.

[41] Defense Institute of Security Cooperation Studies, "International Training," *Green Book*, January 2017.

funding data by manually pulling data from SANWeb into a spreadsheet and matching them with data that the DSCA comptroller has pulled from DFAS.[42]

To compile detailed information on the students trained through CTFP-funded programs, the courses attended, and assessments of their effectiveness, the DSCA program manager relies on input from the designated CTFP managers at the CCMD level who are assigned to manage the proposal and data-collection process for the program.[43] The CTFP managers are able to reach out directly to the SCOs who have firsthand knowledge of each country in their AORs to gather information. They also train the SCOs to ensure that they know how to properly manage and record data on the CTFP program.

This best practice has enabled the CTFP program to improve its compliance with congressional requirements. Still, it has not provided a means of automating the collection of financial information on disbursements or a means of coordinating or validating the data the CTFP program managers collect with the data other DoD communities collect. Data collected for the FMTR, for example, are published on a different schedule than the data published in the CTFP annual report.

Cooperative Threat Reduction

Congress established the CTR program in 1991 to assist former Soviet states in securing and dismantling their stockpiles of nuclear weapons to prevent the proliferation of WMD.[44] Subsequent legislation expanded the program to address the proliferation of chemical and biological weapons and outbreaks of diseases throughout Asia, Africa,

---

[42] There are approximately 3,000 fund entries in SANWeb that program managers work with financial analysts to reconcile to prepare their annual report. Discussions with DoD officials, August 2016.

[43] Some CTFP management positions are combined with the International Military Education and Training program.

[44] The CTR program is often referred to as the Nunn-Lugar program, after Senator Richard Lugar and former Senator Sam Nunn, who sponsored the original legislation that created the program included in the Soviet Nuclear Threat Reduction Act in November 1991, P.L. 102-228.

and the Middle East. DoD's authority to assist countries in addressing these wide-ranging threats was then codified under the DoD Cooperative Threat Reduction Act in 2014 (part of the FY 2015 NDAA, P.L. 113–291) to become 50 USC, Ch. 48.[45]

The reporting requirements outlined in 50 USC, Ch. 48, are among the most extensive of any security cooperation program. They include notifying Congress of proposed activities prior to the obligation of funds and submitting annual reports that include information on estimated expenditures for the year and proposed spending over the course of a five-year plan (corresponding with DoD's Future Years Defense Program). These detailed reports must also describe all activities and assistance carried out under the program during the previous FY, including the amount of funds obligated and expended for each activity by country, the objectives of the activity, and an assessment of its success. The title further requires a description of the means used to ensure that assistance provided under the program is fully accounted for, used for its intended purpose, and used efficiently and effectively.[46]

There are a number of barriers to collecting such detailed data, not the least of which is that funding allocations for the CTR program are made in a manner similar to that for the CN program, with funds designated by Congress for a specific purpose rather than a country. For CTR, these purposes are the elimination of strategic arms, chemical weapon destruction, global nuclear security, cooperative biological engagement, proliferation prevention, threat reduction engagement,

[45] 50 USC, War and National Defense, governs how the United States declares and conducts wars and how it ensures national security. This title includes intelligence operations, as well as military equipment and nuclear security. Parts of the CTR program that had been included under 22 USC (Foreign Relations and Intercourse) and 10 USC (Armed Forces) were combined by P.L. 113-291 Section 1311 in 2014 in 50 USC Ch. 4. The FY 2017 NDAA (P.L. 114–328) does not consolidate the CTR with other security cooperation programs; however, some of its counter-WMD activities may be subsumed under the new multipurpose authority to build capacity of foreign security forces. The implications are not clear at the time of this writing.

[46] 50 USC 3743, Reports on Activities and Assistance Under Department of Defense Cooperative Threat Reduction Program.

and other assessments.[47] As a result, money allocated for activities in particular countries or regions is often reprogrammed and therefore difficult to track. Funding obligations are made with a three-year period in which the funds can be spent, which makes tracking on an FY cycle difficult. And as with other security cooperation programs, financial data are managed separately from program data.

The CTR program has a unique administrative structure, however, which allows closer coordination between program and financial offices. While OSD Policy—through the DASD for Countering WMD and Office of the Assistant Secretary of Defense for Acquisition, Technology, and Logistics' Nuclear, Chemical, and Biological Defense Programs—provides strategic guidance and oversight for the program (in much the same way that OSD's SO/LIC office oversees many security cooperation programs), DTRA serves as both the program manager and implementing agency for the CTR program. This allows DTRA to maintain responsibility for managing the program, allocating funds, and administering contracts, which provides it with greater access and control over CTR activities and funding.[48] Moreover, the CTR program also maintains its own dedicated financial and contracting offices within DTRA, which are physically colocated and linked administratively through the regular sharing of information. This enables closer collaboration between communities.

For reporting purposes, DTRA has been able to develop an effective way to integrate program and financial data. Financial information on each CTR activity is tracked within DTRA's database, which draws from the Defense Agencies Initiative (DAI), with a country code

---

[47] 50 USC 3711, Authority to Carry Out Department of Defense Cooperative Threat Reduction Program.

[48] DTRA manages approximately 300 to 400 contracts of varying types each year. It also develops long-term implementation strategies, program plans, and budgets for the DoD CTR Program; develops technical requirements with the ministries and agencies of the recipient states; and manages the performance, cost, and schedule of CTR projects. It is responsible for tracking data, which it submits to OSD Policy through the Office of the Assistant Secretary of Defense for Acquisition, Technology, and Logistics' Nuclear, Chemical, and Biological Defense Programs. The policy office is responsible for interaction with Congress and issues the final congressional report.

and a CTR designation, or a unique identifier, and is carried through on every MIPR and contract.[49] The same identifiers are used within DTRA's Work Breakdown Structure, which tracks programs and pulls data into a common spreadsheet, referred to as the Program Budget Management Tool (PBMT), located on a SharePoint site. Although data are pulled together manually, they are reconciled weekly to ensure their accuracy. The PBMT is a common point of reference for all offices that are completing external reports and conducting internal program reviews; as DoD officials noted, this ensures that they "all always talk from the same page."

The linkages between the financial and program management data made by the PBMT database have enabled DTRA to collect the detailed information it requires for its annual reports and most of the data needed to satisfy DoD's Foreign Assistance Dashboard requirements. The types of information the financial databases capture have limitations, however. Travel costs for military-to-military events are tracked separately, for example. Moreover, the manual process of pulling data from financial and management systems is onerous and labor-intensive, making it very difficult for DTRA to be able to be able to provide comprehensive reports more frequently than once a year, as the Foreign Assistance Dashboard (and the FY 2017 NDAA) requires. While there have been some efforts to automate data collection, none has been implemented to date. Table 3.2 provides an overview of the barriers for CTR and the other four security cooperation programs.

Summary of Innovative Workarounds

Our analysis of the OHDACA, GT&E, CN, CTFP, and CTR programs indicates that, while there are significant barriers to gathering comprehensive program and financial data on security cooperation programs, a number of notable practices have also been developed to

---

[49] The 10 to 20 percent of CTR activities that are allocated to a region, rather than a country, do not receive identifiers and are manually reconciled. A MIPR is a method of transferring funds from one military organization to another to procure services, supplies, or equipment.

Table 3.2
Overview of Barriers by Program

	OHDACA	GT&E	CN	CTFP	CTR
Patchwork of authorities	Five different authorities with different requirements	Reporting requirement for notification and assessment only	Authorities do not differentiate between operational and foreign assistance activities	Annual report not on FY cycle	Includes Title 50 activities beyond scope of security cooperation
Separate planning, program, and financial communities	Planning databases do not track disbursement of funding	Training tracked on ad hoc basis, separate from equipment	Program office has little visibility into how CN funds are used	Funding data not linked to SANWeb	DRTA-run, separate from other security cooperation programs
Financial data not consistently defined, tracked, or reported	Only obligations of funds to geographical CCMDs are required to be reported	Lacks process for validating data	CN database does not track activity-level data	SANWeb tracks estimated costs or obligations not disbursements	Allocations can be reprogrammed; quarterly obligations difficult to track

meet existing reporting requirements. These practices have been helpful in providing data to the Foreign Assistance Dashboard and may be useful in meeting the requirements under the new FY 2017 NDAA. Not surprisingly, we found that, across these five programs, the programs with the most extensive congressional reporting requirements had developed the most extensive and effective workarounds.

Table 3.3 illustrates how past congressional requirements have driven more detailed reporting by color coding against four criteria we assessed were important for facilitating transparency: (1) the comprehensiveness of existing congressional reporting requirements, (2) the extent of linkage between communities, (3) the level of detail of data collected, and (4) the degree to which databases integrate program and financial data. For each program, we looked the type of data required to be reported, which varied from the most general listing of total obligations and number of missions conducted during the FY to more-specific data on both obligations and expenditures on individual activities within a particular country. We examined the processes or mechanisms that linked programing and financial communities, which ranged from informal engagements in the proposal process to prescribed weekly meetings of program, financial, and contracting staff operating within the same agency. We also looked the data collected for each program, which included information on project plans and estimated costs and more-detailed information on and assessments of executed activities. Finally, we examined databases that were being used to track program and financial data. Some of these databases, such as OHASIS, provided for some integration of program and financial data for the proposal process, while others, such as the CN database, incorporated more data on program expenditures.

The degree of comprehensiveness, the extent of the linkages, level of detail, and the degree of integration were evaluated as low, medium, or high, with light blue indicating a relatively low level, medium blue indicating a moderate level, and dark blue indicating a comparatively high level. The comparison of the five programs is by no means an indication that one program is better managed or has a higher degree of compliance than another, only that some programs have been required to meet more stringent requirements and were able to find a way to

Table 3.3
How Select Security Cooperation Programs Meet Current Congressional Reporting Requirements

	OHDACA	GT&E	CN	CTFP	CTR
Comprehensiveness of reporting requirements	Total obligations Number of missions	Notifications Assessments	Biannual expenditures by country and activity type	Expenditures by country and activity After-action reports	Notifications Obligations, expenditures, and plans by country and activity
Degree of linkage between communities	Proposal process	Case adjustment process	DoD Inspector General's report	CTFP Manager	DTRA connections
Level of detail of data collected	Projects planned Estimated costs CCMD allocations	Building partner capacity cases Equipment delivery Training	CN activity by country Project code	Students, courses by country, assessments	Planned, executed activities by country
Degree to which databases integrate program and financial data	OHASIS	SCIP SANWeb	CN Database	SANWeb	PBMT SharePoint

SOURCE: Discussions with DoD officials.

NOTES: Dark blue indicates greatest level of detail required for congressional reporting, most significant linkages between communities, comprehensive data collection on disbursements, or highest degree of integration of program and financial data, depending on the row.

do so. All programs were able to meet their congressionally mandated reporting requirements. The benefit of comparing the five programs is simply to demonstrate the differences that exist between security cooperation programs and the various mechanisms that have been developed to gather better data.[50] The table is intended to provide an overview of some effective practices that have been developed over time, although, ultimately, such workarounds can only go so far. As reporting requirements become more stringent, it will be necessary to adopt more-comprehensive solutions for security cooperation reporting.

The table notes that OHDACA, which is required only to report on total obligations and number of humanitarian assistance in its annual reports, has placed a greater emphasis on collecting data for the proposal process and has therefore developed a system for collecting detailed data on security cooperation projects and estimated costs from the CCMDs through OHASIS. The GT&E program, which requires reporting on notification and assessments, has developed closer linkages between the planning, program management, and financial communities and better data collection through its pseudo-FMS case adjustment process. The program also has developed ways to integrate data during this process through SCIP and SANWeb.

The CN program requires more-extensive biannual reporting on expenditures and has adopted a means of creating greater linkages between the program and financial offices by requesting an annual DoD Inspector General review of its reporting. It has also developed a specialized database to track CN activities by type and country using project codes. The CTFP program, which has even-more-comprehensive requirements, has engaged a CTFP manager at each of the CCMDs to collect detailed data from the SCOs who have the best access to detailed country-level data. Finally, the CTR program, which has the most comprehensive reporting requirements but also a unique administrative structure, has created close linkages between program and financial management by physically integrating the two

[50] In fact, the chart may help to demonstrate that those programs that have had less stringent congressional reporting requirements in the past may face more difficult hurdles to meeting ForeignAssistance.gov and 2017 reporting requirements in the future.

offices and maintaining responsibility for all contracting activities. It also developed an effective, although still manual, means of integrating activity-level data on its PBMT SharePoint website.

While none of these best practices are an ideal model for simplifying the security cooperation data process, they together offer examples of possible techniques for tracking data from the CCMDs and the SCOs, coding activities by country, and integrating data from program and financial databases more systematically. A combination of these techniques may be adopted in the future to collect and validate data security cooperation data.

It is important to emphasize that our research did not point to an obvious technical solution for streamlining the security cooperation data process. Some DoD officials mentioned that G-TSCMIS, which is intended to serve as the primary information system for managing security cooperation activities across the CCMDs, would be a logical starting point for developing a new process; yet across the board, we heard that G-TSCMIS itself could not provide the means of linking activity-level program and financial data. Recognizing these limitations, we recommend that DoD consider adopting a combination of the tools DoD program managers and other U.S. agencies currently use, as will be discussed in the next chapter.

CHAPTER FOUR

Lessons from Department of State and USAID Transparency Efforts

The challenge of collecting data on U.S. assistance to foreign countries is not unique to DoD. Most government agencies have difficulty meeting open data requirements, IATI standards, and broader internal reporting requirements. DoS and USAID experience many of the same challenges as DoD in collecting foreign assistance data for the Foreign Assistance Dashboard, although neither agency must differentiate between foreign assistance and security cooperation or protect classified information on U.S. engagements with partner nations that are linked to military operations. However, the process of data collection within DoS and USAID is similarly complicated by the difficulties of protecting sensitive information and by complex authorities; bureaucratic divisions between planning, program, and financial communities; a lack of consistency across financial accounting systems; and the fact that reported data that are neither reconciled or verified.

Over the past several years, DoS and USAID have made a concerted effort to address issues of transparency in response to OMB's Open Government Directive in 2009 and its "Guidance on Collection of U.S. Foreign Assistance Data of 2012" (Bulletin 12-01[1]) by initiating their own Open Government Plan and FADR.[2] We undertook a literature review of U.S. open government efforts, particularly DoS and USAID transparency efforts, and engaged in a series of discus-

[1] OMB, 2012.

[2] Orszag, 2009.

sions with USAID and DoS officials to learn about their transparency efforts. We found that both agencies have made progress through these efforts; while both contend that they have a long way to go to develop comprehensive, automated data collection systems, these efforts provide some valuable lessons learned for DoD.[3]

USAID Transparency Efforts and IATI Cost Management Plan

USAID initiated an agency-wide effort to improve transparency in reporting in 2009 in response to OMB'S Open Government Directive and has focused particularly on improving its contributions to the Foreign Assistance Dashboard and IATI through its open government plans in subsequent years. In an effort to gain their input and support for the effort, the agency began with a major effort to engage its leadership in the process of improving transparency and socializing the effort with all the bureaus to explain the new reporting requirements, the types of data that would become publicly available, and what safeguards would be in place for redaction.[4]

As a result of its concentrated effort, USAID became the first U.S. government agency to publish obligation and disbursement data by operating unit and sector to IATI in 2012 and the first to release disaggregated transaction-level data to the Foreign Assistance Dashboard in 2013. It provided a total of 75,000 records to the dashboard, including spending data that connect financial information across 30 qualitative

---

[3] We also reviewed reports of similar efforts by the Millennium Challenge Corporation. While this corporation and other agencies have undertaken significant internal transparency efforts, we chose to focus on DoS and USAID because the barriers they face in reporting are most similar to DoD's.

[4] It is important to note that USAID's initial efforts to socialize the transparency process were not entirely successful, as data inputs intended for internal accounting purposes were published on the Foreign Assistance Dashboard without sufficient internal awareness. This problem was later addressed by reviewing data before they were released. Discussion with U.S. government officials, officials, August 8, 2016.

fields.[5] Moreover, the 2015 *IATI Cost Management Plan* enabled the agency to make considerable progress delivering on its IATI commitments and make substantial improvements in its PWYF ATI score.[6] To produce its cost management plan, USAID established a small technical working group. This working group included IT personnel and budget and program management staff to gather information on data management systems. Together, the members of the group identified reporting gaps and explored the feasibility and complexity of reporting on each additional Foreign Assistance Dashboard and IATI element. They then identified and discussed all areas of possible improvement and conducted an informal cost-benefit analysis that weighed the level of complexity against expected results. This included for example, the degree of effort and costs necessary to make structural changes, conduct technical work, or introduce system upgrades.[7]

The working group then outlined a four-phased approach, which began identifying immediate gains in compliance (or "quick wins" to improve its PWYF score) that USAID could achieve with minimal additional effort using its existing manual collection process. It then outlined possible changes to the agency's reporting process to streamline its submissions to the Foreign Assistance Dashboard, which could potentially improve transparency scores more substantially. This second phase focused on developing a browser-based tool that would allow a direct data pull from certain USAID corporate financial and project management systems to begin automating the data collection process.[8] The tool required the creation of common terms and program identification codes that could be used across various corporate systems. During the third phase, a plan was made to establish an automated

---

5 USAID, *Open Government Plan 3.0*, Washington, D.C., 2014, p. 4.

6 USAID, 2015b.

7 USAID, 2015b.

8 According to USAID reports, all data reported to IATI had been shared manually from Excel spreadsheets. The new automated system was to draw data from USAID's Phoenix financial system, the Global Acquisition and Assistance System, Foreign Assistance and Coordination Tracking System (FACTS Info), and Development Experience Clearinghouse program management systems. See USAID, 2015b.

process for the redaction of sensitive information. USAID reviewers were to be provided with a web interface on a secure server to process redaction requests, rather than relying on manually sharing spreadsheets.[9] Then, during the fourth phase, changes were to be made to the source systems themselves to provide more comprehensive and timely data. This would involve changing procedures for inputting data into existing systems and could lead to the adoption of a new information system to collect and publish data.

By FY 2016, USAID was able to implement the first three phases of the *IATI Cost Management Plan*, which resulted in the agency making significant improvements in the quality and quantity of the data it reported to IATI.[10] The agency added 21 additional fields to its quarterly reporting to the Foreign Assistance Dashboard, which increased the agency's level of IATI compliance. This also resulted in an improvement of 20 points (on a 100-point scale) in the agency's score in PWYF's 2015 Aid Transparency Review, moving it from the "Fair" to the "Good" category between 2014 and 2015.[11] In the 2016 Aid Transparency Review, USAID's score of 59.1 percent dropped back just enough to move the rating back to fair because of the omission of some basic activity-level information, such as titles and descriptions. Yet the agency still maintained an 18-point increase over the 2014 score, leading PWYF to commend USAID for its continued improvement in data quality.[12] At the same time, the agency was able to demonstrate improvements in its internal reporting systems with the Development Information Solution, which is currently in development.[13]

---

[9] This process enabled USAID to audit changes to redaction rules and to track reviewers who were delinquent (USAID, 2015b).

[10] Wade Warren, "USAID Continues to Deliver on Aid Transparency," USAID Blog, April 13, 2016.

[11] USAID, 2015b. PWYF, "2015 U.S. Aid Transparency Review," 2015.

[12] PWYF, "2016 U.S. Aid Transparency Review," 2016a.

[13] Warren, 2016.

Department of State's Foreign Assistance Data Review

DoS initiated its own targeted effort to improve the transparency in its foreign assistance reporting with the establishment of a FADR in September 2014. The FADR was conducted by a working group that represented a cross section of DoS program and financial offices, including offices of Foreign Assistance Resources, Management and Resources, Comptroller, and Information Management, as well as its functional and regional bureaus. The working group was tasked to understand why DoS

> captures foreign assistance activity from budget planning and allocation through obligation and disbursement in multiple budget, financial, and program management systems . . . [yet] does not utilize these systems effectively to track or report on foreign assistance programs or funds at the level needed for transparency, congressional, or management purposes

and to recommend a path forward.[14]

While the FADR was initially chartered to fulfill transparency needs for the Foreign Assistance Dashboard, the working group determined that it would be better prepared to meet current and future transparency mandates if it focused first on meeting internal requirements, such as budget formulation, budget execution, and intra-agency monitoring and reporting.[15] Members of the working group focused on gathering information on the current systems that the department used to track foreign assistance data during the first phase of the review. Over the course of eight months, the group identified and studied 19 systems, including FACTS Info, which is similar to OHASIS or DSAMS; Global Financial Management System (GFMS), which is similar to DFAS; and the Regional Financial Management System (RFMS), which has some similarity to service accounting systems.[16]

---

[14] DoS, 2015, p. 1.

[15] DoS, 2015, p. 1.

[16] DoS, 2015, Append. 6.2, p. 29.

Not surprisingly, the initial FADR Findings Report published in 2015 found that DoS's "multiple budget, financial, and program management systems. . . . were not designed to track or report on these foreign assistance programs or funds at the level demanded by internal and external stakeholders."[17] This was confirmed by DoS officials, who noted that, while detailed information on foreign assistance programs was captured by individual embassies and bureaus, these data were not consistently tracked in DoS's management systems. Moreover, the type of financial data required to be reported to the Foreign Assistance Dashboard did not exist in financial systems. The report concluded that it would be necessary, in subsequent phases, to establish a standard set of foreign assistance data elements and processes across the department to identify foreign assistance system requirements needed to collect these data elements and, finally, to implement an integrated system solution.[18]

During phase two of the FADR process, completed in 2016, the working group determined that it would not be feasible to establish a single standard business process across all bureaus, given their unique data requirements, and instead focused on incorporating standard data elements into existing bureau processes.[19] It then reached an agreement on common definitions for 57 key fields that could be used for budget and programmatic offices across the department and aligned these fields with the data elements in the Foreign Assistance Database and other external reporting required by the Digital Accountability and Transparency Act and the Foreign Aid Transparency and Accountabil-

---

[17] DoS, 2015, p. 6. The Inspector General's report had a similar conclusion, that "The Department's core financial system programs—GFMS and RFMS—meet many of the Department's needs. However, efforts to facilitate tracking and managing of foreign assistance programs and related reporting have been piecemeal" (DoS, Office of the Inspector General, "Management Assistance Report—Department Financial Systems Are Insufficient to Track and Report on Foreign Assistance Funds," February 26, 2015).

[18] It became clear that attempting to introduce a single process would not only be more costly and time consuming but might also unnecessarily affect processes designed to address other bureau-specific needs. DoS, 2016, p. 22.

[19] DoS, 2016, p. 4.

ity Act.[20] These 57 key fields, referred to as the FADR Data Element Index, in turn, helped the working group identify the extent to which data were being captured by enterprise-wide information systems and where there were gaps.

In a future phase three, the working group planned to determine the requirements for updating DoS's information systems to address these gaps. In phase four, it would then implement an "integrated systems solution" that could produce more comprehensive public reporting.[21]

Although the DoS FADR is an ongoing process, and officials note that it has yet to develop an effective means of integrating program data, the FADR working group has made progress in identifying key data elements required for external reporting and aligning these elements across data systems.[22] The working group process has also allowed closer integration of financial and program managers as they work together on a weekly basis to create new categories of data that fall across information systems. Moreover, the FADR process has been applied to existing systems; DoS officials noted that they "can't afford to build a multimillion dollar system."[23]

---

[20] Working group members engaged both financial and program management functions within their offices to identify data elements currently available in single-entry account systems but not yet captured by enterprise-wide systems. As part of this process, the working group outlined the 11 funding phases that foreign assistance funds move through and the type of information produced during each phase. The phases examined covered department-level budget planning through execution and program closeout. This was done to understand when and where data gaps are introduced into the enterprisewide information management systems and what standard information would need to be collected to close these gaps. However, the process did not finalize any crosswalks required to compare data across different enterprise systems. This was left for a later phase. DoS, 2016, pp. 5–6.

[21] The process of sorting through these different definitions of and perspectives on data fields and arriving at standardized definitions required approximately eight months of negotiation and concentrated effort on the part of the diverse, cross-departmental working group.

[22] According the 2016 FADR report, the DoS working group determined that it was highly unlikely that a single standard business process could sufficiently meet bureau needs; however, the group was able to begin incorporating a standard set of data elements into existing bureau processes to allow some degree of standardization without restricting processes that address specific bureau foreign assistance. DoS, 2016.

[23] Focused discussions with U.S. government officials June 29, 2016.

Department of State Data Warehouse

In addition to the FADR process, DoS has undertaken an ongoing effort to develop a data repository to improve its collection of financial data for foreign assistance reporting. This system, known as the GFMS Data Warehouse, is managed by the DoS Comptroller and is populated by transactional data drawn from the department's enterprisewide financial system. All DoS transactions include U.S. Treasury codes that link transactions to a specific authority or funding source and allow financial analysts to pull data and generate reports according to their funding source.[24] The warehouse is currently the main source of financial data for all external and most internal reporting.[25]

To enable meaningful reporting on foreign assistance, transaction data in the data warehouse includes award identifiers (unique numbers that are assigned to each foreign assistance activity or transaction) that are aligned with corresponding award identifiers within DoS's FACTS Info. Although these award identifiers divide data by sector rather than by country, they provide a critical link between program and financial data. Using Treasury codes and award identifiers, a designated budget analyst within the comptroller's office is able to pull data from the data warehouse to create a customized financial report on DoS foreign assistance transactions. This data file is then combined with FACTS Info program data files to produce a single, integrated file, which is then manually reconciled to produce a single data report.

While the data warehouse represents significant progress in producing automated data reports, the process remains incomplete. Linking the financial transactions to operational plans hinges on the award identifier; occasionally, these do not line up and need to be linked

[24] Treasury codes do not appear to be used as consistently in DoD accounting. A review of DoS reporting on the Foreign Assistance Dashboard shows that each of DoS's 152,926 reported transactions includes U.S. Treasury account codes; in contrast, only 798 of DoD's 2634 transactions—less than one-third—include these codes. This was based on RAND's gap analysis, which assessed the extent to which DoD is reporting on the IATI Standard (see Chapter Two).

[25] It is important to note that U.S. Treasury codes do not identify particular countries, only broad authorities.

manually. Moreover, there is often lack of consensus on what constitutes an award.[26] More fundamentally, award identifiers are sector specific and do not allow data to be divided by country, which is critical to meeting Foreign Assistance Dashboard and IATI requirements. Finally, the DoS data warehouse is currently limited to capturing data from the department's GFMS accounting system, which includes only domestic transactions and a summary of overseas transactions. It does not pull data from RFMS, the contract management system, or the System for Award Management governmentwide grant system. While there are plans to extend the warehouse further in the future, it has to date failed to capture significant amounts of spending on foreign assistance activities.

Nonetheless, the process of developing the warehouse has substantially improved data linkages and communication between the different communities. DoS officials note that one of the biggest successes was getting members of the programming and financial communities "speaking the same language." In particular, the dialogue between the comptroller and the program managers revealed where common or needed data elements were already collected but called different things.[27]

Department of State and USAID Transparency Efforts Provide Important Lessons for DoD

In conclusion, while USAID and DoS are still working to improve processes to automate data collection, pull from all financial systems, code data by country, and verify data submissions, the transparency efforts of both agencies clearly provide some important lessons for DoD. Having placed a high priority on improving data collection and reporting processes since 2009, they have found ways to incentivize cooperation; improve the coordination between planning, program-

---

[26] Discussion with DoS officials, August 9, 2016; discussion with data warehouse team, November 15, 2016.

[27] Discussion with DoS officials, June 29, 2016.

ming, and financial communities; and implement new capabilities for data management that may be instructive to future DoD efforts. Some of the most significant lessons are as follows:

- Socializing transparency requirements with both senior leadership and staff is important to gaining buy-in. Both USAID and DoS promoted transparency as an agencywide effort intended not only to meet Foreign Assistance Dashboard and IATI requirements but also to improve mission effectiveness.[28] The two agencies spent time ensuring that new processes were linked with existing processes to reduce the reporting burdens on staff and that program officers were able to use the foreign assistance data that they collected. The two agencies also emphasized that principled exceptions were permitted to protect sensitive information from being publicly released and that bureau offices vet all data.
- The working group model can bring together the necessary programming, budgeting, and IT expertise to address complex data-collection problems. While both the USAID technical working group and the DoS FADR working group required a significant investment of staff time, they proved critical to uncovering the various sources of foreign assistance data and discovering ways to link data from different systems. As one government official noted, "there is an advantage to having different stakeholders together in the same room; in some instances, the group spontaneously came up with solutions to the problems being discussed."[29]
- Defining reporting requirements and developing clear definitions is the first step. The first task of the working groups was to define "foreign assistance" and to determine what accounts were required to be reported to the Foreign Assistance Dashboard. The FADR working group spent a considerable amount of time identifying such terms as *financial pipelines*, which had various meanings even within a single agency. Key terms need to be commonly

[28] USAID noted specifically that having a champion at the executive level was essential when prioritizing transparency. Discussions with U.S. government officials.

[29] Discussion with U.S. government officials, September 2016.

understood to ensure that reported data are comparable and consistent.

- Developing a common coding system is difficult but essential to collecting consistent and reliable data. Program identification codes are necessary for USAID to implement data pulls. Award identifiers allow data to be tracked by sector in the DoS data warehouse. Both agencies continue to work on improving their coding systems and ways to crosswalk data across systems to integrate data.

Improving transparency is a multistep process. USAID and DoS have developed a phased effort to improve data collection and reporting that is extending over several years and appears to be taking even longer than anticipated. The main lesson appears to be that, even with concerted and well-resourced efforts, adopting new mechanisms for data collection and reporting takes time.

CHAPTER FIVE

Findings and Recommendations

As U.S. funding for security cooperation activities has increased over the past decade, there has been a corresponding demand for greater transparency to demonstrate where and how DoD has engaged with its partners and how these activities benefit U.S. national security interests. In this report, we have focused on the reporting requirements of the Foreign Assistance Dashboard and IATI and have delineated a number of other external drivers for transparency that have arisen from open government directives and congressional reporting requirements. We have also noted that there are equally pressing needs within the Pentagon to obtain better data on security cooperation funding and, indeed, on defense spending as a whole for the purposes of policy planning, resource management, and prioritization in the development of future security cooperation strategy.[1] In fact, we consistently heard from officials both inside and outside DoD that these internal motivating factors will likely drive the considerable effort it would take to address the seemingly insurmountable barriers to collecting comprehensive data on DoD's security cooperation programs.

These barriers are the result of many factors, including the patchwork of authorities on which DoD security cooperation programs are derived. The barriers are a reflection of the stovepiping of planning, programming, and management offices engaged in the administra-

[1] It should be reiterated that the barriers to collecting data are not unique to security cooperation programs but reflect a systematic accounting problem that extends throughout DoD (Scott J. Paltrow, "As Trump Seeks Defense-Spending Boost, Watchdogs Cite Faulty Pentagon Accounting," Reuters, April 13, 2017).

tion of security cooperation programs. Moreover, they represent the inherent challenges of tracking and reporting financial data, including the difficulty of identifying which financial data to collect, establishing visibility across the different accounting systems in which the data reside, and linking information on disbursements with and programmatic data. The last challenge is complicated by the fact that there are currently no common codes or identifiers that can be used to connect financial data with their programs, which has prevented program systems of record, such as G-TSCMIS and OHASIS, from drawing on authoritative financial data sources. The data currently being entered into these systems are submitted manually by planners and typically include only estimated, projected spending.

Security cooperation program managers have been able to adopt a number of practices to overcome these barriers to collecting data on disbursements and meeting existing reporting requirements. While these practices will not be sufficient to meet the more expansive and detailed reporting of the FY 2017 NDAA, they may provide useful guidelines for the development of a new reporting system. The informal linkages that have been developed across offices, integration of SCOs in the data-collection process, and use of coding mechanisms to integrate program management and financial data may prove to be particularly valuable inputs to this process.

Transparency efforts that USAID and DoS have undertaken since 2009 also provide lessons that could be incorporated into a future reporting system. USAID's methods of tracking transactional-level data, DoS's use of a data warehouse, and using working group processes to develop a greater commitment to transparency and improve foreign assistance reporting are notable examples of the insights that can be drawn from other agencies. While there is clearly no easy means of addressing the many barriers DoD faces in tracking security cooperation programs, our analysis of U.S. efforts to meet IATI requirements, DoD best practices, and USAID and DoS lessons learned may provide some insight into the process of integrating program and financial data through the use of common codes to improve security cooperation reporting.

Recommendations

This research was intended to illuminate the DoD's process for collecting and reporting on its security cooperation engagements and to recommend the first steps preliminary first steps toward improving transparency. Our recommendations are based on a review of five DoD programs and discussions with a cross section of officials engaged in security cooperation and foreign assistance reporting. These recommendations may serve as a guide for future analysis but are not a substitute for a more comprehensive survey of security cooperation programs and stakeholders. For example, our discussions with USAID and DoS provided evidence of the value of a systematic transparency effort but did not validate the effectiveness of the working group model at DoD or offer a definitive solution for collecting and reporting data. Moreover, while we uncovered various program and financial databases used to collect security cooperation information, this research was not intended to offer specific technical solutions for linking these databases. These issues, which are beyond the scope of our study, will need to be addressed at a later stage.

Short-Term Recommendations to Improve Transparency in Security Cooperation Reporting

In the short term, we recommend that DoD strengthen the current process of security cooperation reporting, provide clearer definitions and consistency in the data being reported using existing sources, and begin to align tasks for meeting IATI and new NDAA requirements. The majority of these recommendations are directed at OSD, more specifically to the Office of the DASD for Security Cooperation, which in 2016 had the primary role in collecting and reporting data to the Foreign Assistance Dashboard. The specific short-term recommendations are as follows:

- **Define the scope for DoD security cooperation transparency.** To ensure that both internal and external audiences understand the scope of DoD's reporting requirements to the Foreign Assistance Dashboard and IATI and the limits of its reporting, DoD officials should clarify, in policy guidance, congressional reporting, and other documents, that security assistance activities constitute a subset of both U.S. foreign assistance and DoD security cooperation activities and that there are restrictions on the releasability of some data due to exceptions for national security. Agency notes about the Foreign Assistance Dashboard can be used to state that, while foreign assistance is defined as activities that provide tangible or intangible benefits to a partner nation, security cooperation is defined more broadly to include all DoD's interactions with foreign security partners for building partner capacity, establishing access, and promoting relationships for specific U.S. security interests. It should be clearly stated that some of DoD's engagements in security are not designed to benefit a partner directly. Therefore, not all security cooperation activities will be reported as foreign assistance. Relatedly, DoD officials should work with Foreign Assistance Dashboard and congressional staffers to develop reasonable expectations for DoD reporting based on current data availability. While improvements can be expected on the collection of country-level data, it may not be possible to obtain the level of detail required for all DoD security cooperation activities by 2018. Finally, due to U.S. national security concerns and the sensitivity of foreign partners, not all foreign assistance data can be made available to the public.

- **Focus on improving DoD's ability to aggregate and validate existing data** before seeking new data sources. While there is pressure for DoD to provide more data for the Foreign Assistance Dashboard and to provide information on activity-level disbursements in FY 2017, DoD should focus first on collecting existing country-level data on obligations by program and reporting the data as accurately as possible. OSD has made a considerable effort to engage with offices across DoD to gather existing data, much of which is currently in annual reports to Congress. Before expanding further, more progress can be made in validating the data provided and ensuring that it is consistent with the information published by other government sources, such as the Foreign Aid Explorer, the FMTR, and congressional budget documents.

This effort would provide more credible data on the Foreign Assistance Database in FY 2017 and provide the basis for more consistent DoD reporting in the future.

- **Develop a process for vetting security cooperation data** to determine what data can be released to the public or made available to external websites. This process may involve submitting information to country desks and program officers in a manner similar to DoS's submission of foreign assistance data to its bureau offices.
- **Build a shared reporting template for all offices to submit security cooperation data** by following the model developed by DTRA and its PBMT SharePoint site. To provide more-consistent data input, OSD could create a single online site for all DoD offices to provide security cooperation information to be submitted to the Foreign Assistance Dashboard. This process would help DoD move toward reporting data on a quarterly basis and may provide a means of reconciling data more regularly. Ultimately, the use of such a shared online spreadsheet may provide a means of integrating program and financial data.
- **Align data collection for the Foreign Assistance Dashboard with the broader security cooperation data required by the FY 2017 NDAA.** This will require DoD to seek a clarification of business rules for more data collection for FY 2018. DoD would benefit from discussions with DoS Foreign Assistance Dashboard representatives and possibly congressional staffers on the definitions of data ranges and terms (such as what qualifies as an obligation, commitment, or disbursement) to minimize uncertainty in the collection and reporting process. It will also require discussions on how to crosswalk data identifiers to align data inputs with the Foreign Assistance Dashboard and IATI and the time lines for collecting and reporting data to ensure inputs are aligned with congressional requirements. Progress made in defining business rules for collecting more-detailed data that apply to both the Foreign Assistance Dashboard and the NDAA will not only make the process more efficient but will reduce the number of requests

for security cooperation data, which could alleviate some of the burden on DoD program and financial managers.

- **Work with Foreign Assistance Dashboard and congressional staffers to develop reasonable expectations for DoD reporting based on current data availability.** While improvements can be expected on the collection of country-level data, it may not be possible to obtain the level of detail required for all DoD foreign assistance or security cooperation activities by 2018. It may be more reasonable to expect incremental improvements in data reporting.
- **Launch a policy-level working group to address future reporting requirements.** It will be of utmost importance for DoD to get the right people around the table to improve DoD's security cooperation data-management process and begin to develop new reporting standards. Using the model USAID and DoS developed for their transparency efforts, a policy-level working group should engage financial, program, and information management offices; the Joint Staff; and DSCA to establish a common understanding of the value of greater transparency and discuss existing barriers to collecting comprehensive data and possible IT solutions (and investments) that may be needed to overcome these barriers. Discussions should include ways to incorporate activity data tracked by G-TSCMIS with resource data collected through DoD financial systems. Such a working group would be useful for obtaining policy-level input, support, and buy-in for a multiple-stage process for developing an integrated system to comply with both IATI and the FY 2017 NDAA and, more important, to enable DoD to meet critical internal reporting requirements.

By taking the first step toward integrating the data-collection process and developing a method for validating and vetting security cooperation information, OSD can improve DoD's submissions to the Foreign Assistance Dashboard and prepare for the more-comprehensive reporting the FY 2017 NDAA requires. It can further aid in this process by beginning to align current and future requirements for foreign assistance and security cooperation programs and establishing a policy-level working group to provide the necessary support and resources for future systemwide efforts to improve security cooperation program tracking and reporting.

Longer-Term Recommendations to Prepare for FY 2017 NDAA Reporting Requirements

For the longer term, DoD will need to both plan and implement the significant changes required to track and report security cooperation programs more effectively. This will need to be done within the context of the new security cooperation program management structure outlined in the FY 2017 NDAA, which designates DSCA as the agency "responsible for the execution and administration of all security cooperation programs and activities" and for submitting quarterly monitoring reports to Congress.[2] Our long-term recommendations therefore focus on DSCA, which will be experiencing a major expansion of its portfolio and will likely assume the primary role meeting these new reporting requirements. The following are the specific recommendations:

- **Allocate more internal resources to DSCA as it takes on a more significant role in consolidating security cooperation administrative and reporting processes.** DSCA already manages a number of Title 10 security cooperation programs (including OHDACA, GT&E and CTFP); however, this currently constitutes a small portion of its administrative work and budget, which is dominated by Title 22 security assistance and sales. The implementation of the FY 2017 NDAA will require the agency to shift more of its attention toward Title 10 programs while taking on a much larger administrative burden. DSCA will undoubtedly need to increase its capacity to manage additional programs. The agency would benefit from consolidating the administrative and reporting processes that currently exist and from incorporating the best practices other organizations have developed. Given the short time line for implementing the administrative changes,

---

[2] FY 2017 NDAA (P.L. 114–328), §382, "Execution and Administration of Programs and Activities."

it may be most expedient to delegate the responsibility for managing and reporting on some programs, as the NDAA explicitly allows.[3] The CTR program, which is based on Title 50 authorities and has an independent administrative structure under DTRA, may be an example of a program that could be managed separately. Management and reporting functions for the CN program may also be delegated, at least temporarily, to OSD to ensure that it maintains the benefits of its unique CN database and its coding system, which may ultimately serve as a model that could be incorporated across programs. In the medium term, however, DSCA should work with these organizations to develop a plan to transition at least reporting responsibilities to DSCA, so that senior DoD leaders and other stakeholders can finally develop an integrated picture of security cooperation return on investment.

- **Establish standing working groups to develop common reporting standards and mechanisms for collecting and reporting security cooperation program data.** We recommend that DSCA institutionalize linkages between the program, financial, and information management communities and begin to engage key stakeholders in the development of new reporting standards and data-collection processes. It may be helpful to build on the OSD working group recommended above by establishing working groups within each of the CCMDs to create better links between program offices, implementing agencies, and SCOs to develop more effective mechanisms for collecting transaction data by country. This process also helps participants recognize how such data would be useful to them in carrying out their duties. DSCA could organize these groups to complement working groups established at the policy level by OSD, as recommended above.

[3] According FY 2017 NDAA (P.L. 114–328), p. 514, the DSCA director "may designate an element of an armed force, combatant command, Defense Agency . . . to execute and administer security cooperation programs and activities . . . if the Director determines that the designation will achieve maximum effectiveness, efficiency, and economy in the activities for which designated."

- **Ensure that all accounting systems speak the same language** when tracking security cooperation funding. The DSCA comptroller could lead an effort to develop consistent financial data requirements for security cooperation programs and common identifiers for transactions across military departments, agencies, and contractors. This herculean task may be aided by DSCA's adoption of DAI, which is expected to streamline financial management capabilities and may allow the introduction of common identifiers for transactions across military departments, agencies and contractors.[4]
- **Incorporate common business rules for security cooperation reporting** by establishing country codes that can be used across financial and program systems. An effective tracking system will require all offices to use the same coding system for reporting on security cooperation activities. The development of new coding systems may be coordinated with the new DAI system. The Joint Staff's J6 Directorate (Command, Control, Communications and Computers/Cyber) may also be to assist in developing new coding mechanisms.
- **Define new roles for staff to manage data collection at the regional and country level.** To achieve the level of detailed reporting Congress requires, greater visibility into activity-level information is necessary. Currently, most of this information resides at the country level with the SCOs or at the regional level with implementing agencies. CCMDs, implementing agencies, and SCOs will need to provide insight into the additional manpower and resources necessary to collect more-comprehensive data. For example, DSCA may benefit from positioning a data coordinator at each CCMD who could operate in much the same way as the CTFP coordinator.
- **Establish a central location for financial data** modeled on the DoS's data warehouse. DSCA could assign a dedicated budget

---

[4] DAI is an effort across the DoD enterprise to modernize the financial management processes for many DoD agencies by streamlining financial management capabilities, addressing financial reporting material weaknesses, and supporting financial statement auditability.

analyst to pull financial data on its security cooperation programs using common identifiers that could later be reconciled with program management data. This process could be used to issue reports for all internal and external audiences to ensure more consistency in the publication of program funding. Moreover, it could eventually lead to the development of a more automated system for reconciling program and financial data.

- **Consider IT solutions for linking program and financial data.** One option would be to develop a software or web tool that would allow data from DoD accounting systems to be matched to data collected through DoD's G-TSCMIS. A two-step system could adopted that would allow financial analysts to verify the data pulled from DoD accounting systems before it is matched with program data in a more automated fashion using the software tool. Another option would be to engage in a more comprehensive effort to redesign the G-TSCMIS system to serve both a program and financial management function and allow for both offices to input data simultaneously.

Congress has called for significant changes in the way security cooperation programs are managed and reported, with DSCA assuming responsibility for implementing the majority of these changes. We recommend that DSCA use this transition to institute a new structure for collecting security cooperation data. Because these changes are taking place at the same time that DoD is incorporating DAI, it may be possible for DSCA to leverage the capabilities of the DAI to implement more comprehensive changes in security cooperation reporting.

Conclusion

Designing an effective mechanism to collect and report comprehensive data on DoD's security cooperation programs is a major challenge. It will require a multistage planning process involving stakeholders from throughout the DoD enterprise. This process will undoubtedly require the expenditure of manpower and resources and, perhaps most important, will require a commitment to tracking security cooperation programs to meet internal and external requirements. While congressional and other external requirements will drive the effort to get better data, the utility of this data to DoD stakeholders will likely determine how effective the process will be. The ultimate goal for these stakeholders should be to understand the return on security cooperation investments. DoD leaders and planners who can put resources into the activities that provide the greatest bang for the buck will be most effectively supporting U.S. national security objectives. Following the money in security cooperation may be the critical first step in capturing security cooperation data and demonstrating the value of transparency in day-to-day operations and in long-term strategy, planning, programming, and resourcing decisions.

Suggestions for Further Research

This report provides the initial analysis of possible ways to overcome the current barriers to collecting security cooperation funding data. Further research is clearly needed to map out the reporting processes of all DoD's security cooperation programs (particularly those that will be combined under the FY 2017 NDAA) and to depict all the various data systems that are currently being used. It will be important to obtain the perspectives of a wider range of offices and implementing agencies engaged in collecting data to develop an effective approach to meeting new transparency requirements. It would be valuable to engage further with various DoD stakeholders from the planning, programming, financial, and information management communities in working group discussions to find ways to map out new reporting processes. These working groups could be held at the OSD, DSCA, and CCMD levels.

Additional research is needed to determine how to pull financial data from DoD's various accounting systems and to reconcile this data. OSD and the DSCA comptroller could be engaged in a more in-depth study focusing on how best to utilize DAI to meet new security cooperation reporting requirements. Such a study would benefit from a thorough review of DoD accounting practices and the work that the agency has done in preparation for the FIAR plan.[5]

Greater consideration should also be given to developing effective web tools to enable DoD to automate the process of data collection and reporting. A more in-depth analysis could be undertaken to explore the possibility of pulling data from accounting systems and linking it with G-TSCMIS or other tracking tools. Such a study would involve both data managers and IT experts, as well DoD financial managers and personnel engaged in recording security cooperation data in the field.

Finally, because much of the problem of security cooperation reporting relates to knowledge management, it would be valuable to conduct a review of literature on knowledge management and engage in a more in-depth analysis of DoD's knowledge-management processes. This would not only provide a better context for the obstacles DoD faces in meeting its security cooperation reporting requirements but also help to provide insight into the most comprehensive solutions for addressing DoD transparency issues more broadly.

---

[5] For more information on the FIAR, see Office of the Under Secretary of Defense (Comptroller)/Chief Financial Officer, *Financial Improvement and Audit Readiness (FIAR) Plan Status Report*, Washington, D.C.: U.S. Department of Defense, May 2016.

Abbreviations

AOR	area of responsibility
ATI	Aid Transparency Index
CCMD	combatant command
CN	counternarcotics
CN&GT	Counternarcotics and Global Threats
CT	counterterrorism
CTFP	Combating Terrorism Fellowship Program
CTR	Cooperative Threat Reduction
DAI	Defense Agencies Initiative
DASD	Deputy Assistant Secretary of Defense
DFAS	Defense Finance and Accounting Service
DoD	U.S. Department of Defense
DoS	U.S. Department of State
DSAMS	Defense Security Assistance Management System
DSCA	Defense Security Cooperation Agency
DTRA	Defense Threat Reduction Agency

FACTS Info	Foreign Assistance and Coordination Tracking System
FADR	Foreign Assistance Data Review
FIAR	Financial Impact and Audit Readiness
FMS	Foreign Military Sales
FMTR	Foreign Military Training Report
FY	fiscal year
GAO	U.S. Government Accountability Office
GFMS	Global Financial Management System
GT&E	Global Train and Equip Program
G-TSCMIS	Global Theater Security Cooperation Management Information System
IATI	International Aid Transparency Initiative
IT	information technology
MIPR	Military Interdepartmental Purchase Request
NDAA	National Defense Authorization Act
NGO	nongovernmental organization
OHASIS	Overseas Humanitarian Assistance Shared Information System
OHDACA	Overseas Humanitarian, Disaster, and Civic Aid
OMB	Office of Management and Budget
OSD	Office of the Secretary of Defense
P.L.	Public Law
PBMT	Project Budget Management Tool

PWYF	Publish What You Fund
RFMS	Regional Financial Management System
SANWeb	Security Assistance Network Web Tool
SCIP	Security Cooperation Information Portal
SCO	security cooperation officer
SO/LIC	Special Operations and Low Intensity Conflict office
USAID	U.S. Agency for International Development
USC	U.S. Code
WMD	weapons of mass destruction
XML	Extensible Markup Language

References

Defense Institute of Security Cooperation Studies, "International Training," *Green Book*, January 2017. As of January 18, 2017:
http://www.iscs.dsca.mil/documents/greenbook/14_Chapter.pdf

Defense Security Cooperation Agency, "Humanitarian Assistance, Disaster Relief and Mine Action," information paper, Washington, D.C., July 2012. As of December 20, 2016:
http://www.dsca.mil/sites/default/files/ohdaca.pdf

———, "Fiscal Year 2016 Budget Estimates: Overseas Humanitarian, Disaster, and Civic Aid," Washington, D.C., February 2015a. As of June 17, 2016:
http://comptroller.defense.gov/Portals/45/Documents/defbudget/fy2016/budget_justification/pdfs/01_Operation_and_Maintenance/O_M_VOL_1_PART_2/Volume_I_Part_II.pdf

———, *Historical Facts Book: Foreign Military Sales, Foreign Military Construction Sales and Other Security Cooperation Historical Facts*, Washington, D.C., September 30, 2015b. As of June 22, 2017:
http://www.dsca.mil/resources/dsca-historical-facts-book-fiscal-year-series

———, "Security Cooperation Information Portal: SCIP Background," January 2016a. As of March 8, 2017:
http://www.disam.dsca.mil/documents/greenbook/v34_1/20_Appendix_1_EDITION34_1_150911.pdf

———, *Fiscal Year 2017 President's Budget Defense Security Cooperation Agency (DSCA): Overseas Humanitarian, Disaster, and Civic Aid*, Washington, D.C., February 2016b.

———, *Security Assistance Management Manual*, Washington, D.C., 2017. As of March 7, 2017:
http://www.samm.dsca.mil/chapter/chapter-12#C12.4

Department of Defense 7000.14-R, *Department of Defense Financial Management Regulation*, various dates. As of June 13, 2017:
http://comptroller.defense.gov/FMR.aspx

Department of Defense Directive 5132.03, *DoD Guidance for Security Cooperation*, Washington, D.C.: U.S. Department of Defense, August 29, 2016.

Department of Defense Instruction 5132.14, *Assessment, Monitoring, and Evaluation Policy for the Security Cooperation Enterprise*, January 13, 2017. As of March 6, 2017:
http://www.dtic.mil/whs/directives/corres/pdf/513214_dodi_2017.pdf

DoS—*See* U.S. Department of State.

DSCA—*See* Defense Security Cooperation Agency.

Ellis, Jr., James O., James N. Mattis, and Kori Schake, "Restoring Our National Security," in George P. Shultz, ed., *Blueprint for America*, Stanford, Calif.: Hoover Institution, 2016, pp. 137–150. As of March 6, 2017:
http://www.hoover.org/research/blueprint-america

Foreign Assistance Dashboard, website, undated. As of March 8, 2017:
http://foreignassistance.gov/

ForeignAssistance.gov, "About Aid Transparency," webpage, undated. As of June 9, 2017:
http://foreignassistance.gov/learn/about-aid-transparency

ForeignAssistance.gov, "FA.gov Data Dictionary," June 27, 2017. As of June 27, 2017:
http://foreignassistance.gov/assets/data-dictionary.xlsx

FY 2017 NDAA—*See* Public Law 114–328.

GAO—*See* U.S. Government Accountability Office.

Global Washington, "Foreign Assistance Dashboard—Bringing More Transparency to US Foreign Aid," GlobalWA website, December 23, 2010. As of June 13, 2017:
http://globalwa.org/2010/12/foreign-assistance-dashboard/

IATI—*See* International Aid Transparency Initiative.

International Aid Transparency Initiative, "About IATI," webpage, undated a. As of June 12, 2017:
http://www.aidtransparency.net/about

———, "Dashboard," webpage, undated b. As of March 8, 2017:
https://iatiregistry.org/registry-dashboard

———, homepage, undated c. As of March 7, 2017:
http://iatistandard.org/201/

———, "IATI Standard: Guidance," webpage, undated d. As of June 17, 2016:
http://iatistandard.org/202/guidance/

———, *IATI Annual Report*, 2015. As of March 7, 2017:
http://www.aidtransparency.net/annualreport2015/downloads/IATI_Annual_Report_2015.pdf

Joint Chiefs of Staff, *The National Military Strategy of the United States of America 2015*, Washington, D.C.: U.S. Department of Defense, June 2015. As of June 9, 2017:
http://www.jcs.mil/Portals/36/Documents/Publications/2015_National_Military_Strategy.pdf

Marquis, Jefferson P., Michael J. McNerney, S. Rebecca Zimmerman, Merrie Archer, Jeremy Boback, and David Stebbins, *Developing an Assessment, Monitoring, and Evaluation Framework for U.S. Department of Defense Security Cooperation*, Santa Monica, Calif.: RAND Corporation, RR-1611-OSD, 2016. As of June 8, 2017:
http://www.rand.org/pubs/research_reports/RR1611.html

Marquis, Jefferson P., David E. Thaler, S. Rebecca Zimmerman, Megan Stewart, and Jeremy Boback, *The Global-Theater Security Cooperation Management Information System Assessment and Implications for Strategic Users*, Santa Monica, Calif.: RAND Corporation, 2016, Not available to the general public.

Modernizing Foreign Assistance Network, "MFAN Statement: Sec. Clinton Speech in Busan Reaffirms U.S. Commitment to Aid Effectiveness," November 30, 2011. As of April 18, 2017:
http://modernizeaid.net/2011/12/mfan-statement-sec-clinton-speech-in-busan-reaffirms-u-s-commitment-to-aid-effectiveness/

Moroney, Jennifer D., David E. Thaler, and Joe Hogler, *Review of Security Cooperation Mechanisms Combatant Commands Utilize to Build Partner Capacity*, Santa Monica, Calif.: RAND Corporation, RR-413-OSD, 2013. As of June 8, 2017:
http://www.rand.org/pubs/research_reports/RR413.html

FY 2017 NDAA—*See* National Defense Authorization Act for Fiscal Year 2017.

Office of Management and Budget, "Guidance on Collection of U.S. Foreign Assistance Data," Washington, D.C., Bulletin 12-01, September 25, 2012.

Office of the Under Secretary of Defense (Comptroller)/Chief Financial Officer, *Financial Improvement and Audit Readiness (FIAR) Plan Status Report*, Washington, D.C.: U.S. Department of Defense, May 2016. As of April 19, 2017:
http://comptroller.defense.gov/Portals/45/documents/fiar/FIAR_Plan_May_2016.pdf

OMB—*See* Office of Management and Budget.

Organisation for Economic Co-operation and Development, "Paris Declaration and Accra Agenda for Action," undated. As of June 21, 2017:
http://www.oecd.org/dac/effectiveness/parisdeclarationandaccraagendaforaction.htm

Orszag, Peter R., "Open Government Directive," memorandum for the heads of executive departments and agencies, Washington, D.C., December 8, 2009. As of June 21, 2017:
https://obamawhitehouse.archives.gov/open/documents/open-government-directive

Paltrow, Scott J., "As Trump Seeks Defense-Spending Boost, Watchdogs Cite Faulty Pentagon Accounting," Reuters, April 13, 2017. As of April 20, 2017:
http://www.reuters.com/article/us-usa-trump-pentagon-idUSKBN17F1PQ?utm_source=Sailthru&utm_medium=email&utm_campaign=EBB%20 4.14.17&utm_term=Editorial%20-%20Early%20Bird%20Brief

Public Law 87–195, Foreign Assistance Act of 1961, as amended through P.L. 115–31, May 5, 2017

Public Law 101-501, Augustus F. Hawkins Human Services Reauthorization Act of 1990, November 3, 1990.

Public Law 102-228, Soviet Nuclear Threat Reduction Act of 1991, December 12, 1991.

Public Law 103-337, National Defense Authorization Act for Fiscal Year 1995, October 5, 1994.

Public Law 105–85, National Defense Authorization Act for Fiscal Year 1998, November 18, 1997.

Public Law 106-398, Floyd D. Spence National Defense Authorization Act for Fiscal Year 2001, October 30, 2000.

Public Law 109-163, National Defense Authorization Act for Fiscal Year 2006, January 6, 2006.

Public Law 111-84, National Defense Authorization Act for Fiscal Year 2010, October 28, 2009.

Public Law 112-239, National Defense Authorization Act for Fiscal Year 2013, January 2, 2013.

Public Law 113-110, Digital Accountability and Transparency Act of 2014, May 9, 2014.

Public Law 114–92, National Defense Authorization Act for Fiscal Year 2016, November 25, 2015.

Public Law 114-191, Foreign Aid Transparency and Accountability Act of 2016, July 15, 2016. As of June 23, 2017:
https://www.congress.gov/bill/114th-congress/house-bill/3766/text

Public Law 114–328, National Defense Authorization Act for Fiscal Year 2017, December 23, 2016.

Publish What You Fund, "2015 U.S. Aid Transparency Review," 2015.

———, "2016 U.S. Aid Transparency Review," 2016a. As of January 11, 2017: http://ati.publishwhatyoufund.org/wp-content/uploads/2016/04/2016-U.S.-Aid-Transparency-Brief.pdf

———, "Aid Transparency Index: 2016 Index," 2016b. As of January 6, 2017: http://ati.publishwhatyoufund.org/wp-content/uploads/2016/02/ATI-2016_Report_Proof_DIGITAL.pdf

———, "Aid Transparency Index: 2016 U.S. Brief," 2016c. As of January 6, 2017: http://ati.publishwhatyoufund.org/wp-content/uploads/2016/04/2016-U.S.-Aid-Transparency-Brief.pdf

PWYF—*See* Publish What You Fund.

Ross, Tommy, "Leveraging Security Cooperation as Military Strategy, *Washington Quarterly*, Fall 2016.

Security Assistance Monitor, "Defense Bill Breakdown: Key Military Aid Issues in the FY 2017 National Defense Authorization Act," September 26, 2016. As of January 25, 2017:
http://securityassistance.org/fact_sheet/defense-bill-breakdown-key-military-aid-issues-fy-2017-national-defense-authorization-act

Serafino, Nina, *The Department of Defense Role in Foreign Assistance: Background, Major Issues, and Options for Congress*, Washington, D.C.: Congressional Research Service, RL34639, December 9, 2008. As of December 20, 2016:
https://fas.org/sgp/crs/natsec/RL34639.pdf

Thaler, David E., Michael J. McNerney, Beth Grill, Jefferson P. Marquis, and Amanda Kadlec, *From Patchwork to Framework: A Review of Title 10 Authorities for Security Cooperation*, Santa Monica, Calif.: RAND Corporation, RR-1438-OSD, 2016. As of June 8, 2017:
http://www.rand.org/pubs/research_reports/RR1438.html

Tran, Mark, "Hillary Clinton Declares US Support for Aid Initiative," *Guardian*, November 30, 2011. As of April 18, 2017:
https://www.theguardian.com/global-development/2011/nov/30/hillary-clinton-aid-initiative-busan

U.S. Agency for International Development, "Foreign Aid Explorer," website, undated. As of June 13, 2017:
https://explorer.usaid.gov/aid-dashboard.html

———, *Open Government Plan 3.0*, Washington, D.C., 2014.

———, "Aid Transparency Country Pilot Assessment," Final Report, Washington, D.C., May 2015a. As of June 17, 2016:
https://www.usaid.gov/sites/default/files/documents/1870/AidTransparencyCountryPilotAssessment.pdf

———, *International Aid Transparency Initiative (IATI) Cost Management Plan*, Washington, D.C., June 2015b. As of January 11, 2017:
https://www.usaid.gov/documents/1870/usaid-iati-cost-management-plan

USAID—*See* U.S. Agency for International Development.

USASpending.gov, website, 2017. As of June 13, 2017:
USASpending.gov

USC—*See* U.S. Code.

U.S. Code, Title 6, Domestic Security.

U.S. Code, Title 10, Armed Forces.

U.S. Code, Title 10, §333, Foreign Security Forces: Authority to Build Capacity.

U.S. Code, Title 10, §345, Regional Defense Combating Terrorism Fellowship Program

U.S. Code, Title 10, §401, Humanitarian and Civic Assistance Provided in Conjunction with Military Operations.

U.S. Code, Title 10, §402, Transportation of Humanitarian Relief Supplies to Foreign Countries.

U.S. Code, Title 10, §404, Foreign Disaster Assistance.

U.S. Code, Title 10, §407, Humanitarian Demining Assistance and Stockpiled Conventional Munitions Assistance: Authority; Limitations.

U.S. Code, Title 10, §2249c—See U.S. Code, Title 10, §345.

U.S. Code, Title 10, §2282, Authority to Build the Capacity of Foreign Security Forces

U.S. Code, Title 10, §2561, Humanitarian Assistance

U.S. Code, Title 10, Ch. 16, Security Cooperation.

U.S. Code, Title 22, Foreign Relations and Intercourse.

U.S. Code, Title 50, War and National Defense.

U.S. Code, Title 50, Ch. 4, Espionage.

U.S. Code, Title 50, Ch. 48, Department of Defense Cooperative Threat Reduction.

U.S. Code, Title 50, §3711, Authority to Carry Out Department of Defense Cooperative Threat Reduction Program. As of January 18, 2017:
https://www.law.cornell.edu/uscode/text/50/3711

U.S. Code, Title 50, §3743, Reports on Activities and Assistance Under Department of Defense Cooperative Threat Reduction Program. As of January 18, 2017:
https://www.law.cornell.edu/uscode/text/50/3743

U.S. Department of Defense, Inspector General, *Independent Auditor's Report on the FY 2015 DoD Detailed Accounting Report for the Funds Obligated for National Drug Control Program Activities*, Alexandria, Va., DODIG-2016-041 January 29, 2016. As of June 13, 2017:
http://www.dodig.mil/pubs/documents/DODIG-2016-041.pdf

U.S. Department of Defense and U.S. Department of State, *Joint Report to Congress, Foreign Military Training and DoD Engagement Activities of Interest (FMTR)*, Washington, D.C., 2016. As of June 22, 2017:
https://www.state.gov/t/pm/rls/rpt/fmtrpt/

U.S. Department of State, *Foreign Assistance Data Review: Findings Report*, December 2015. As of June 17, 2016:
https://www.state.gov/documents/organization/250931.pdf

———, *Foreign Assistance Data Review: Phase Two—Data Element Index*, Winter 2016. As of June 9, 2017:
https://www.state.gov/documents/organization/267146.pdf

U.S. Department of State, Bureau of the Comptroller and Global Financial Services, *Fiscal Year 2014 Agency Financial Report*, November 2014. As of June 17, 2016:
https://www.state.gov/documents/organization/234331.pdf

U.S. Department of State, Office of the Inspector General, "Management Assistance Report—Department Financial Systems Are Insufficient to Track and Report on Foreign Assistance Funds," February 26, 2015. As of June 22, 2017:
https://oig.state.gov/system/files/isp-i-15-14.pdf

U.S. Government Accountability Office, *Humanitarian Development Assistance: Project Evaluation and Better Information Sharing Needed to Manage Military's Efforts*, Washington, D.C., February 2012. As of March 7, 2017:
http://www.gao.gov/assets/590/588334.pdf

———, *DoD Financial Management: Greater Visibility Needed to Better Assess Audit Readiness for Property, Plant, and Equipment*, Washington, D.C., GAO-16-383, May 2016a. As of April 19, 2017:
http://www.gao.gov/assets/680/677471.pdf

———, *Foreign Assistance: Actions Needed to Improve Transparency and Quality of Data on ForeignAssistance.gov*, Washington, D.C., GAO-16-768, August 2016b. As of June 17, 2016:
http://www.gao.gov/assets/680/679204.pdf

———, *High-Risk Series: Progress on Many High-Risk Areas, While Substantial Efforts Needed on Others*, Washington, D.C., GAO-17-317, February 2017. As of April 19, 2017:
http://www.gao.gov/assets/690/682765.pdf

Warren, Wade, "USAID Continues to Deliver on Aid Transparency," USAID Blog, April 13, 2016. As of December 19, 2016:
https://blog.usaid.gov/2016/04/usaid-continues-to-deliver-on-aid-transparency/